Physical Characteristics of the Bouvier des Flandres

(from the American Kennel Club breed standard)

Back: Short, broad, well muscled with firm level topline.

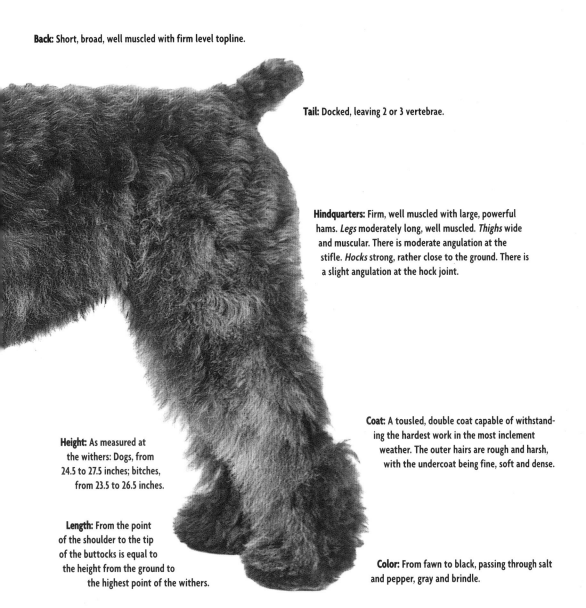

Tail: Docked, leaving 2 or 3 vertebrae.

Hindquarters: Firm, well muscled with large, powerful hams. *Legs* moderately long, well muscled. *Thighs* wide and muscular. There is moderate angulation at the stifle. *Hocks* strong, rather close to the ground. There is a slight angulation at the hock joint.

Coat: A tousled, double coat capable of withstanding the hardest work in the most inclement weather. The outer hairs are rough and harsh, with the undercoat being fine, soft and dense.

Height: As measured at the withers: Dogs, from 24.5 to 27.5 inches; bitches, from 23.5 to 26.5 inches.

Length: From the point of the shoulder to the tip of the buttocks is equal to the height from the ground to the highest point of the withers.

Color: From fawn to black, passing through salt and pepper, gray and brindle.

Bouvier
des Flandres

By Dr. Robert Pollet

Contents

Training Your Bouvier des Flandres   **105**

Begin with the basics of training the puppy and adult dog. Learn the principles of house-training the Bouvier des Flandres, including the use of crates and basic scent instincts. Get started by introducing the pup to his collar and leash and progress to the basic commands. Find out about obedience classes and other activities.

Healthcare of Your Bouvier des Flandres   **126**

By Lowell Ackerman DVM, DACVD
Become your dog's healthcare advocate and a well-educated canine keeper. Select a skilled and able veterinarian. Discuss pet insurance, vaccinations and infectious diseases, the neuter/spay decision and a sensible, effective plan for parasite control, including fleas, ticks and worms.

Showing Your Bouvier des Flandres   **150**

Step into the center ring and find out about the world of showing pure-bred dogs. Here's how to get started in AKC shows, how they are organized and what's required for your dog to become a champion. Take a leap into other competitive events: obedience, agility, tracking and herding.

GUSS

KENNEL CLUB BOOKS: BOUVIER DES FLANDRES
ISBN: 1-59378-297-7

Copyright © 2005 • Kennel Club Books, LLC
308 Main Street, Allenhurst, NJ 07711 USA
Cover Design Patented: US 6,435,559 B2 • Printed in South Korea

10 9 8 7 6 5 4 3 2 1

Photography by Carol Ann Johnson
with additional photographs by

D. Abras, Paulette Braun, T.J. Calhoun, Alan and Sandy Carey, Carolina Biological Supply, David Dalton, Karl Donvil, Isabelle Français, Bill Jonas, Dr. Dennis Kunkel, Tam C. Nguyen, Phototake, Dr. Robert Pollet, Jean Claude Revy, Ruud Vinck and the Belgian dog magazine *Woef*.

Illustrations by Patricia Peters.

Special thanks to the NBC (Nederlandse Bouvier Club) for supplying the photos of Dutch champions and to the owners of the dogs featured in this book.

The breed's name derives from the word *bouvier*, which means "cow-herder" in French. A beautiful example of the modern Bouvier des Flandres is Belg. Ch. Noska von Gewdraa Oel.

HISTORY OF THE
BOUVIER DES FLANDRES

The exact origins of many breeds have never been documented or are said to be buried in history, because these breeds already existed centuries before any interest in "pure-bred dogs" began. For other breeds, their actual histories can be traced and their evolutions can be documented easily. Fortunately, with the Bouvier des Flandres much information is available on the breed's beginnings and early history, although it is still rather difficult to trace the exact origin of the breed.

WHAT'S IN A NAME?
The word *bouvier* translates from the French to mean a person who tends bovines; therefore, it means "cow-herder" and, as a derivation, also "cow dog." This has the same meaning as the Dutch *Koehond*. Mostly, when using the name "Bouvier," it is the Bouvier des Flandres to which one is referring, although there are many other breeds that are used as cattle dogs.

Many characteristic Flemish names have been given to the Bouvier des Flandres, such as "Boever" (from the French

bouvier); "Pikhaar" (pick hair) or "Pik," which refers to the "picking" or rough hair; and "Vuilbaard" (dirty beard), referring, of course, to his beard and mustache, which soak up water when he drinks and become soiled.

WHERE DOES THE BOUVIER COME FROM?
The complete and official name of the breed is Bouvier des Flandres, which is French, meaning "cow or cattle dog of Flanders." In Dutch, the breed is named "Vlaamse

The legendary Nic was of unknown origin but was a military dog and a well-known Belgian champion who died in 1926 and is considered as the founding sire of the Bouvier breed.

BELGIË-BELGIQUE

26

VLAANDERSE KOEHOND BOUVIER DES FLANDRES

1986 (9D) A.B.

BELGIAN BREEDS ON STAMPS

On May 26, 1986, four postage stamps were issued in Belgium to honor the Belgian working breeds. The Bouvier des Flandres and three Belgian Sheepdog breeds—the Malinois, Tervuren and Groenendael—were featured on the stamps.

Koehond" (Flemish cow dog) or "Vlaanderse Veedrijver" (cattle drover of Flanders). As the name indicates, the Bouvier originated in Flanders, which during the Middle Ages was a county that occupied territories of the present-day French *département* of Nord, the Belgian provinces of East Flanders and West Flanders and the Dutch province of Zeeland. Because the Bouvier originated in Flanders, which was Belgian as well as French, the breed is considered to be both Belgian and French. Consequently, both Belgium and France are responsible for maintaining the official Bouvier des Flandres breed standard of the Fédération Cynologique Internationale (FCI), the main kennel club of continental Europe with member countries around the world.

THE CRADLE OF THE BREED: AN ABBEY

It is generally known that monks have given saints' names to certain breeds, such as the St. Bernard and the Belgian breed the St. Hubert Hound (Bloodhound). We know, thanks to the research of Louis Huyghebaert, a major Belgian canine authority, who in 1948 published the history of the Bouvier in the Belgian magazine *L'Aboi* (meaning "The Bark"), stating that the monks of the abbey Ter Duinen were the first breeders of Bouviers. He also states that the Bouviers at that time were too common and too rustic (rough and unrefined) to be given the name of a patron saint.

The abbey Ter Duinen was founded in 1107 in Coxyde, on the western coast of Flanders. It became the biggest and most famous abbey in Flanders. The monks had their own fleet and they imported dogs from England, especially large, gray-brindle, rough-coated sighthounds, said to be Scottish Deerhounds and Irish Wolfhounds. The imported dogs were bred to the regional farm dogs. Through selective breeding, a large rough-coated dog was created: this is thought to be the ancestor of the Bouvier des Flandres. These predecessors of the Bouvier were excellent guard and defense dogs and very able cattle drovers.

THE EARLY BOUVIER: A FARMER'S DOG AND ALL-AROUND WORKER

Until 1900, not much is known about the evolution of the Bouvier des Flandres. He was a general farmer's helper and cattle herder, and we know from people who lived around the turn of the 20th century that the life he led wasn't enviable or happy at all; it was, in fact, quite a miserable life! He had to work night and day, and the tasks he had to perform were arduous and exhausting. He was able to perform his job, thanks to his strength, endurance and weather-proof coat, and, perhaps above all, thanks to his steady character and temperament.

Among the Bouvier's chores were guarding, droving, hauling and churning. As a draft animal,

CANIS LUPUS

"Grandma, what big teeth you have!" The gray wolf, a familiar figure in fairy tales and legends, has had its reputation tarnished and its population pummeled over the centuries. Yet it is the descendants of this much-feared creature to which we open our homes and hearts. Our beloved dog, *Canis domesticus*, derives directly from the gray wolf, a highly social canine that lives in elaborately structured packs. In the wild, the gray wolf can range from 60 to 175 pounds, standing between 25 and 40 inches in height.

he pulled milk and cheese carts and he turned millstones. It is said that the farmers docked the dogs' tails to prevent injury and to make it easier to outfit them with harnesses, which were necessary equipment for draft work. The ears of the Bouvier were cropped in order to show that it was a working dog and not a pet, because at that time only pet dogs were taxed. The Bouvier did not come inside his owner's house—when he wasn't at work, he was a "bandog," kept chained outdoors as a watchdog, a treatment now forbidden by law in his homeland.

CONFIDENT CHARACTER

As to the character of modern-day Bouviers, we find that they are neither shy nor aggressive, but very self-confident. The modern Bouvier is better adapted to life as a social companion and the new requirements of our increasingly less dog-friendly society, but he is certainly not a "softy."

HEAVEN ON EARTH!

The Bouvier's life as a farm dog was miserable and pitiful, the proverbial "dog's life," indeed! Many Bouvier fanciers now complain, "Where has his roughness gone?" They are referring to the breed's roughness of the coat, behavior and character. In earlier days, everything and everybody he encountered were characterized by roughness and rudeness: the country, the weather, the farmer and the work for which he was used. How, then, could he manage all of this and survive? Of course, by being rough himself! But has he now become a "softy"?

In a certain sense, we can admit that the Bouvier has changed indeed, but certainly only to a degree and in part due to his present-day improved living conditions. It is true that his coat became softer along with his character. He is less grim and crude now, and much friendlier, becoming perhaps a family dog first of all. However, we are absolutely sure that he is

Bouviers are no longer used primarily as working dogs, although they retain their working instincts and are willing and able to perform a multitude of tasks. This Bouvier functions as a "collecting dog."

much happier now—he is well fed, well groomed and well cared for. This is his reward for the lives his ancestors endured without complaint, dutifully and willingly performing so many arduous tasks. It is as if the Bouvier has found a slice of "heaven on earth"!

FURTHER EVOLUTION OF THE BOUVIER

Documentation on the origin and the evolution of the breed is very fragmented, but we know that around the turn of the 20th century, before World War I, the Bouvier was crossbred to the

French Ch. Boyard du Bas Berry shows a remarkable head.

TO CROP OR NOT TO CROP?

In the US, dogs in breeds that are traditionally cropped can be shown with either cropped or natural drop ears, as is the case in some European nations. In the UK and Australia, ear cropping has been banned for years, regarded as a useless, cruel procedure. American breeders and judges prefer the stylish look of cropped ears, which they believe give the dog's head a more appealing, eye-catching appearance. Although some uncropped dogs are shown in the US, it is considerably more difficult to win a champion-ship with a natural-eared dog in a breed that usually is cropped. If you do not want your pup's ears to be cropped, you must let the breeder know from the start.

Briard and the Picardy Shepherd (Berger de Picard). Very important was the international show in Brussels on May 21–23, 1910, although the Bouvier breed was represented by only two dogs— the male Rex (Pic x Bella) and the female Nelly (Beer x Sarah)—both owned by Mr. L. Paret from Ghent. They were judged by Mr. L. Huyghebaert, who was duly impressed by the quality of these dogs. In an article published in *L'Aboi* in 1948, 38 years after the show, he still remembered judging these two dogs, commenting on their excellent character and repeating what he had said

Very often, however, they lacked good proportion, and, as for the head, the broad skull and pointed muzzle were not in harmony.

Mr. Moerman was a farmer who lived in Roeselare (Roulers). His Bouviers, the Roulers type, were large dogs, ranging in size from 25.5 to even 27.5 inches, having short bodies and typical heads due to their broad muzzles. On the other hand, they lacked depth of chest and were high on the legs. They were black or black-brindle in color.

For the sake of completeness, we have to mention that a third, but less interesting, type existed. This type also laid the foundation of the modern Bouvier; namely, the Briard type.

There were years of vehement disputes that hindered the development of the breed. The points of controversy involved the texture and color of the coat and the size of the dog. Mr. Paret asserted that the dogs of Moerman (large and black) were "Bouviers de Roulers," but definitely not "Bouviers des Flandres."

All of these types made their contribution to the construction of today's Bouvier—how much exactly is difficult to say, although apparently the rough coat was brought into the breed by the Paret type, and the dark color and compactness (square body, spacious rib cage and strong head) by the Moerman type. It also

decades prior—that the Bouvier should be gruff and rustic in appearance, like a "block" and never elegant. Mr. Paret is considered to have established, with the sire Rex and the dam Nelly, part of the foundation bloodlines of the present-day Bouvier.

During the following years, a variety of types and breed names still existed, although mainly two types were at the fore: namely, the Paret type and the Moerman (Roulers) type. The Paret-type dogs were fawn or gray-brindle with broad chests, round ribs and short heads with wide skulls and pointed muzzles. Their size was between 23.5 and 25.5 inches.

becomes clear that the real origin of the modern Bouvier des Flandres has to be located in what are now the Belgian provinces of West Flanders and East Flanders, where are situated, respectively, the cities of Roeselare (Roulers) and Gent (Ghent).

The confusion and disagreements over the origin and the single desired breed type are also reflected in the development of the standard. The first standards were developed in 1912 by the Belgian Kennel Club (an organization not affiliated with the FCI, which, by the way, also has its headquarters in Belgium), one for the Bouvier des Flandres and one

for the Bouvier de Roulers. Also in 1912, a standard was written by the Société Royale Saint-Hubert for the Bouvier de Roulers. In this standard, black was an allowed color. In 1913, the Bouvier was recognized by the French Société Centrale Canine, but it was not very clear which type of Bouvier they meant.

EFFECTS OF THE WORLD WARS
The World Wars took their toll on the Bouvier, but, fortunately, thanks to dedicated breeders, the breed did survive. The rapid progress following the adoption of the breed standard in 1912 came to a halt with World War I. By

Bouvier bitch Flora Danny v.d. Vanenblikhoeve, Dutch Champion.

1918, almost all Bouvier stock practically had been eliminated, as its native land was a completely devastated war territory. Only a few Bouviers survived. Perhaps we can derive some comfort from the fact that, during this war, the breed was used as a military dog, more precisely as an ambulance dog and messenger dog.

After the war, the reconstruction of the breed was very difficult. At the all-breed shows, only a few Bouviers could be seen. Of special mention, however, is the Olympic Show in Antwerp in 1920, where 16 Bouviers were present, among them the legendary male Nic, who always was placed first and became a Belgian Champion in 1921. Nothing is known about Nic's origin, but we do know that he was owned by a Bouvier fancier living near the city of Poperinge (southern West Flanders) and bought during the war by the veterinarian Captain (later Major) Barbry of the Belgian Army. Nic was trained as a military dog, particularly as a "trench-dog," and served for three years. After the war, he went to the Sottegem Kennel, owned by Major Barbry's brother, and then to the "de la Lys" Kennel, owned by Mr. Gryson. This kennel was the most important during the post-war period, and Ch. Nic, one of the few survivors of World War I, is the most famous ancestor of the breed and considered to be the foundation sire of the modern Bouvier des Flandres. Nic died in 1926, but he left many worthy descendants.

After the war, the disputes and disagreements about the correct type and coat, especially the pressing need to breed and select toward one uniform Bouvier type, did not stop. However, progress was made and on April 25, 1937 a French-Belgian commission, composed of reputable judges from both countries, jointly wrote a very precise standard for the true, one-and-only Bouvier des Flandres.

Unfortunately, the new standard and all of the efforts to put an end to the disputes and controversies did not bring unanimity, and, less than three years later, World War II broke out. This started another period of struggle for survival for the Bouvier. Once again, the devastation to the Bouvier breed was terrible. World-

Romy Tyson Off Soeranda's Home already looks like a champion at nine months of age.

The stud dog Soprano de la Thudinie, bred by Justin Chastel, the architect of the modern Bouvier. The "dog of Chastel's life," Soprano was the pillar of the breed after World War II.

Belgium jointly adopted a single standard, which was accepted by the Fédération Cynologique Internationale in 1965.

JUSTIN CHASTEL AND OTHER MODERN ARCHITECTS OF THE BREED

We feel obliged, in this chapter on the history of the Bouvier, to honor the contributions of some outstanding personalities in the Belgian canine world to the Bouvier des Flandres. First of all, there is Mr. Félix Verbanck, a highly respected international judge and dedicated breeder who was not only a longtime secretary of the Belgian Bouvier club but also a great promoter of the Bouvier. He was a counselor to all Bouvier breeders, including those in the United States. According to Mr. J. Du Mont, Mr. Verbanck truly is the "realizer" of the Bouvier breed.

Mr. Verbanck did not hold back when praising the merits of Mr. Justin Chastel, owner of the Kennel "de la Thudinie." He said that Mr. Chastel had been the creator of the modern Bouvier and that his breeding lines were of such distinctive quality that they had become the standard for breed type. Mr. Chastel entered the Bouvier scene in 1930, when his godfather gave him a gift of a Bouvier. The first Bouvier bearing his kennel name was Lucifer de la Thudinie. In 1943, he produced

wide, the consequences were very serious and the continued existence of the breed became endangered. Nevertheless, once again the Bouvier survived!

The reconstruction of the breed went slowly, but breeders were beginning to make real progress toward correct type. It took a long time before there was unanimity concerning the desired appearance or type of the Bouvier, when the breed rightly could be considered "genetically fixed" (in type). By 1963, breeders' efforts had achieved fruition, as the Bouvier clubs from France and

Soprano de la Thudinie, which, as he says himself, was "the dog of his life." Soprano won a whole series of championship titles.

During the following years, the Bouviers "de la Thudinie" gradually dominated the dog shows and figured in the pedi-grees of the best Bouviers all over the world. Mr. Chastel also became an influential advisor and authority, always emphasizing the working character of the breed. He published his principles and points of view in articles and in his monograph on the breed, enti-

Typical Bouvier head, displayed by Vodka von Gewdraa Oel. Photo courtesy of the Belgian dog magazine *Woef.*

tled *Le Bouvier des Flandres, hier et aujourd'hui* (The Bouvier des Flandres, Yesterday and Today).

Many people these days are concerned about the character of the breed, the soft coats and the excessive trimming of show dogs. Therefore, it is most interesting to read, for instance, the following excerpt from one of Mr. Chastel's articles on the breed's character: "…the Bouvier is nothing of a dandy. His charm resides in great part in his character. Witness the almost human look through shaggy eyebrows! If he lost this quality, what would he have left?"

Another famous breeder, who worked together with Mr. Chastel and who exported many dogs to the US from the early 1960s on, was Félix Grulois, owner of the

Kennel "du Posty Arlequin." This kennel was founded in 1954 and still exists today.

THE BOUVIER DES ARDENNES, A CLOSE RELATIVE

Many Bouvier fanciers do not know that, after 1910, a smaller Bouvier developed—the Bouvier des Ardennes. Like the Flanders dog, the Ardennes is a compactly built and harsh-coated cattle dog, but with naturally standing uncropped ears. In 1948, in an article on the history of the Bouviers, Louis Huyghebaert wrote that this Bouvier, which might also have been called the "little Bouvier," could be regarded as intermediate between the shepherd dog and the heavy and short Bouvier. Some authors have

Bouviers des Ardennes Yrack and Yohda du Maugré.

written in articles that this breed died out, and some even pretend that the breed never existed! This is completely wrong. This Belgian breed, which originated in the Belgian provinces of Liège and Luxembourg, is recognized by the FCI, which published the official standard. Still today, the Bouvier des Ardennes, which is more supple and agile than the Bouvier des Flandres, is used by farmers and shepherds for herding and droving cattle. Most likely, the Bouvier des Ardennes is "the last real cattle dog in active service in Western Europe"—without doubt a most enviable and honorable title!

THE BOUVIER IN NORTH AMERICA

It is said that the first Bouviers des Flandres came to America with returning World War I infantry soldiers, but these dogs had no impact on the history of the breed in the United States. We may assume, however, that over the years immigrants from Belgium, France and Holland took Bouviers to America, but even their possible contribution to Bouvier breeding has not been recorded.

In 1929, the Bouvier des Flandres was officially recognized as a breed by the American Kennel Club (AKC) and admitted to its Stud Book in 1931. The American Bouvier des Flandres Club was established in 1963 and became a member club of the AKC in 1971.

Until World War II, Bouviers were regularly imported from Europe, but the number of registrations was low. The real story of the Bouvier in America began in 1942 with the arrival of Miss Edmée Bowles and her Bouvier, Belco. Miss Bowles, a native of Belgium (born in Antwerp on June 22, 1899), participated in the Resistance during the war and fled from her home because of the German invaders. She had established her "du Clos des Cerbères" Kennel in 1932 in Schilde, near Antwerp, but, upon her arrival in the US, she took up a new life and made her home in Collegeville, Pennsylvania. She is recognized now as the founder of the breed in America.

Male Bouvier des Ardennes, Xoum du Maugré, bred and owned by Yves Dambrain, was Best of Breed at the Eurodog-show, held in Kortrijk, Belgium.

Miss Bowles's kennel name is most original. "Clos" means "an enclosed property," and Cerberus was, in Greek mythology, the three-headed dog that guarded the entrance to the underworld. In French, "cerbère" metaphorically means "severe, unmanageable guardian."

European breeding stock was imported regularly, mainly from Belgium, Holland and France, and the popularity of the breed markedly increased from the late 1960s on, with imports in ever-increasing numbers. The dogs "de la Thudinie" of Justin Chastel were heavily predominant and really shaped, together with the world-famous "du Posty Arlequin" dogs of Félix Grulois, the Bouvier des Flandres in North America. From 1980 on, however, as a consequence of the incredible popularity of the Bouvier des Flandres in Holland, Dutch imports and the Dutch lines became predominant.

In Canada, the first Bouvier litter was registered in 1960, and today the image and reputation of the Bouvier des Flandres in North America are very strong. He is appreciated for his all-around versatility, foremost as a working dog, but also as a show dog and family pet.

We have to mention that one of the best, if not the best, ambassadors and promoters of the Bouvier, certainly in the English-speaking world but also in other countries, is the American breeder, trainer, canine publicist and writer James R. Engel. He established contacts all over the world with notable Bouvier personalities. His efforts for the promotion of the Bouvier, especially as a working dog, are invaluable.

THE BOUVIER DES FLANDRES IN BRITAIN

Although puppies had already been brought to and recorded earlier in Britain, the breed really

---

AMERICAN PARENT CLUB

The American Bouvier des Flandres Club (ABdFC) is the breed's AKC parent club. The club is a wonderful resource for longtime fanciers and newcomers to the Bouvier alike, with the aim of protecting the breed's best interests. To that end, the club serves myriad purposes, including providing a list of their member breeders for potential owners, offering a "beginners' guide" for those considering adding the Bouvier to their lives, supporting health education and research, setting forth breeding ethics for their members, holding specialty shows and events for the breed, keeping track of statistics, awarding dogs for notable achievement, organizing breed rescue and much more. Learn about all of the club's functions by visiting the ABdFC online at www.bouvier.org, where you'll find a wealth of information about the breed and the club itself.

became established in 1972 with significant imports from the famous Kennel "de la Thudinie." In 1980, the Bouvier des Flandres Club of Great Britain was formed and officially recognized by The Kennel Club of England. Bouviers were imported from the Netherlands (from the famous "van Dafzicht" Kennel) and from the United States. From 1981 on, the breed's popularity steadily increased, the number of registrations climbed and more Bouviers were shown regularly. In 1988, the club organized its first character test. The same year, for the first time, Bouviers could earn Challenge Certificates (awards that lead to a British championship) at the Crufts Dog Show, making individuals of the breed eligible to become champions.

THE BOUVIER ON THE CONTINENT

In most countries on the Continent, there was a steady increase in the popularity of the Bouvier des Flandres during the final decades of the 20th century. The breed, of course, is very important in its two countries of origin, Belgium and France, and also extremely popular in the Netherlands.

In Belgium, as to the number of registrations each year, the Bouvier des Flandres is ranked third, directly after the German Shepherd Dog and the Belgian Sheepdog breeds. Recent statistics show approximately 1,100 Bouviers being registered annually. The Belgian Bouvier des Flandres Club, which was founded in 1922, is one of the most active breed clubs in Belgium.

In the Netherlands in the early 1980s, the Bouvier was the most popular breed—more popular than even the ubiquitous German Shepherd Dog, which on the Continent really seemed to be unbelievable. In 1984, more than 10,000 Bouviers were registered. This number gradually decreased, but in recent years the breed still is number five in popularity. Due

The Bouvier des Flandres took Group First at Crufts, England's largest show, in 1998.

to this popularity, the Netherlands began to take a leading position in the worldwide Bouvier community. The Dutch lines and kennels (such as "van Dafzicht," "van de Overstort," "van het Molengat," "van de Vanenblikhoeve" and others) became famous, and a large number of dogs were exported to the US. However, some disputes and problems arose when there seemed to be two Bouvier types, the show dog and the working dog, which differ in character, body structure and coat.

In the early 1970s, judges spoke of the so-called Dutch-type and the French-Belgian-type Bouvier. We think, however, that this "problem" should not be exaggerated. We know that, many years ago, the existing types merged into a single type, the one-and-only Bouvier des Flandres. Moreover, every Bouvier expert has to admit that the Dutch type possesses qualities that are improvements in the breed, and that at the present time many important steps toward unifying the type already have been taken.

In France, the Bouvier is not among the most popular breeds,

POPULARITY AROUND THE WORLD

It is true that the Bouvier is best known in Europe and the US, but he is present as well on other continents. He enjoys great support in the Republic of South Africa, and Australia also has become active in the breed. There also exists a great interest in the breed in many other countries not mentioned here.

and publishes an informative magazine.

In Germany, the number of annual registrations is rather disappointing; specifically, a little more than 200. Nevertheless, many enthusiastic Bouvier fanciers in Germany are promoting the breed through all kinds of activities and through their quarterly club magazine, *Bouvier aktuell*.

In the Scandinavian countries, and in Spain and Italy, the breed is well known and appreciated. Bouvier des Flandres clubs in these countries are active, and specialty shows are organized regularly.

but certainly is highly appreciated, with a very good reputation as both a working and guard dog and a very suitable family dog. The French club is very active

Jespoetnik-Richel van de Vanenblikhoeve, Group-winning Bouvier at the Winners Show in Amsterdam, 1998.

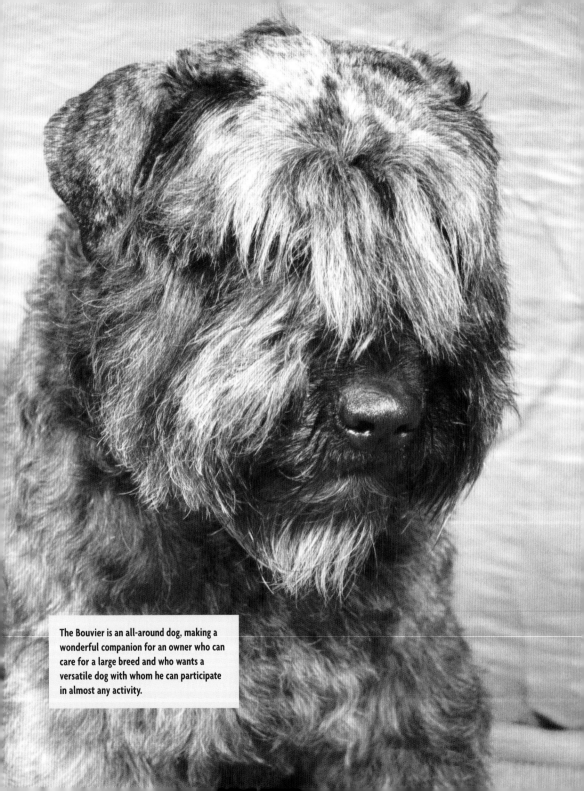

The Bouvier is an all-around dog, making a wonderful companion for an owner who can care for a large breed and who wants a versatile dog with whom he can participate in almost any activity.

CHARACTERISTICS OF THE

BOUVIER DES FLANDRES

Having served humans faithfully for thousands of years, dogs are the most intimate animal companions of man. Over 300 different breeds are recognized today, and all of these breeds share one fundamental virtue, their loyalty to humankind. Nevertheless, each breed certainly has its own personality and characteristics.

The psychology of a breed can be understood best in terms of the work for which it has been selected. The Bouvier des Flandres belongs to the group of cattle dogs. It has always been a working dog, mainly a cattle drover, but without doubt it is an all-around dog that functioned as a livestock and farm guard and that performed an endless variety of tasks. In order to perform all of these arduous tasks, the Bouvier had to be hardy and robust enough to live outdoors in all kinds of weather.

The farmers did not want specialized dogs, but dogs effective as guards and watchdogs, herders, drovers, cart pullers, butter churners and vermin eliminators. In addition, the dogs were

the companions of the farmers' families. The Bouvier also has been used as a military or war dog, more specifically as an ambulance dog and a most successful messenger dog.

Today, the Bouvier is a family dog and a guardian and protector of property, but he still has or should have his original mental and physical characteristics. He can be described as very intelligent; he is not too fast in his reactions, but rather thoughtful. He

The Bouvier is a wonderful guardian of and friend to the family's children, provided they treat each other with care and respect. Here is Qjuero van Gewdraa Oel with a young pal.

is watchful and trainable. These traits, coupled with his physical strength, which is greater than that of the shepherd dog breeds, make him extremely well-rounded. The Bouvier's impressive versatility enables him to perform as a police or service dog, as a tracking dog, as a guide dog for the blind, etc. In addition to his suitability for these professional disciplines, he participates and fares well in all kinds of canine sports, competitions and specialized training.

PHYSICAL TRAITS
To be able to perform effectively as a cattle herder and farmer's helper, the Bouvier requires the physical abilities of a shepherd dog, but in a stronger and more robust form. In modern times, the Bouvier needs these same abilities to be able to function as an all-purpose sports or service dog. As a matter of fact, the physical appearance and traits of the Bouvier are not "lupine" (wolf-like); rather, they are rugged, compact and powerful. He is built as a solid and stable "block," giving an impression of power. However, he is without heaviness, so that suppleness and mobility can be maintained. The head is impressive and the body is broad, short and set on strong-boned and well-muscled limbs.

In the past, Bouviers were bred for their working abilities, but an increasing interest in dog shows made the breeders pay closer attention to appearance. The general appearance of the modern Bouvier des Flandres, especially the show dogs, is very appealing and unique. The "garnish" of the head—specifically, the chin with the rough beard, the upper lip with the heavy mustache and the erect eyebrows—give the gruff expression that is so typical of the breed.

PERSONALITY
The Bouvier is a powerful dog with a highly self-assured personality. His character and virtue are truly his trump cards. His sturdy demeanor sets him apart from other working breeds, sheepdogs or cattle dogs. His strength, endurance, steadiness and well-balanced temperament are very distinctive.

Bouviers are marvelous dogs; still, this is not the perfect breed for everyone! Don't forget that Bouviers were bred to work for the farm family. Their willingness to learn and to please is well known, but they also want to share your home and your life. You will have to pay much attention to your Bouvier puppy from the very beginning. You should train him daily in basic obedience, with brief teaching sessions, so that he is under control at all times. This training is not optional, because a Bouvier needs a real leader. Lack of leadership

During agility testing, a Bouvier clears a jump to retrieve a dumbbell.

and training can cause the dog to develop many bad habits and undesirable behaviors.

Your Bouvier's personality will very probably be enterprising, confident and assertive. A typical Bouvier can be very protective and, more so than other breeds, ready to fight or respond aggressively in situations where he thinks he has to deter intruders and protect his owner's home and family. Only under your leadership will he learn to evaluate situations correctly, so that no regretable incidents happen.

Remember that boredom can be the cause of problems, such as compulsive and/or destructive behaviors. Your Bouvier should never be bored; otherwise, he will look for "work" himself—an occupational pastime that could be very unpleasant or irritating for you. Avoid your Bouvier's becom-

ing bored by doing things with him and keeping him busy. Take your Bouvier on at least one good walk each day on a long lead, or on a retractable lead that allows him even more freedom if he walks politely on a regular lead. If possible, find a suitable enclosed field in which you can allow your Bouvier to run off lead. Go to different places. Your dog will enjoy the outing and the added stimulation of exploring "uncharted territories."

Your Bouvier's need for exercise is average. He will enjoy long walks, but it must be mentioned that Bouviers are rather large dogs and, when your dog is still in his growing phase, he should not be overexerted with too much or too strenuous exercise. A large pen or enclosure, in which the puppy can run, jump and play, as well as rest or sleep in a quiet area when he feels tired, is ideal.

Returning the dumbbell. Photos courtesy of *Woef*.

World Champion Udysee von Gewdraa Oel, showing perfect heeling form. The loose lead indicates that he is neither pulling ahead nor lagging behind. Photos courtesy of *Woef*.

Before considering the drawbacks of the breed, let us first examine the exceptional qualities of the breed's character. The Bouvier is well balanced, which makes him one of the best, if not *the* best, of all herding and cattle-dog breeds. If you are looking for a dog that is by nature an excellent watchdog and guard and, at the same time, an ideal companion or family dog, you have to consider the Bouvier. He is even-tempered, alert, intelligent, willing to please and devoted to his master or mistress. An added "plus" is that all of these qualities are found in an

PROFILE OF THE BOUVIER DES FLANDRES

- **Derivation:** A Flemish breed; its name (Bouvier des Flandres or "Vlaamse Koehond") meaning "cattle or cow dog of Flanders."
- **Place of origin:** Flanders, a former Medieval principality in the southwest of the Low Countries, which occupied a province in the northern part of France, the Belgian provinces of West and East Flanders and the Dutch province of Zeeland.
- **Countries of origin responsible for the breed standard:** Belgium and France.
- **Appearance:** A real cattle dog, blocky, powerful and heavy-boned, with sound legs and square body; structured for strength and endurance; impressive by his stature; reserved and dignified attitude evident.
- **Color:** Generally gray, brindle or smoky; black coat also accepted; pale or washed-out coats are undesirable.
- **Coat:** Very thick, tousled double coat; outer coat rough to the touch on all parts; soft, dense undercoat; the heavy mustache, rough beard and erect eyebrows are distinguishing features, giving forbidding expression.
- **Coat care:** Needs regular grooming.
- **Average weight:** Dogs: 77-88 lb; bitches: 59-77 lb.
- **Average height at withers:** Dogs: 24.5-27.5 inches; bitches: 23.5-26.5 inches.
- **Life expectancy:** Ten to twelve years.
- **Litter size:** Five to ten puppies.
- **Character:** Calm, sensible, serene, stable, laid-back, even-tempered and protective; alert and playful, but also stubborn and reserved.
- **Abilities:** In the past, a cattle drover and general farmer's helper; today, an all-around working and service or police dog, guard and defense dog and family pet.
- **Trainability:** Although highly intelligent, he can be stubborn; responds well to obedience training and can also be trained to high standards in competitive events.
- **Activity level:** Moderate indoors, high outdoors.
- **Dominance:** Toward people and dogs, moderate to high.
- **Sociability:** High with family, but is suspicious of strangers.
- **Children:** Gentle with family children. Children must treat the dog properly.
- **Barking:** Certainly not excessive.
- **Destructiveness:** Low.
- **With other pets:** Gentle if raised together; he is possibly dog-aggressive.
- **Aloofness:** Rather high toward strangers.
- **Aggressiveness:** Low toward family, moderate toward strangers and other dogs, high toward small animals and cats, which he likes to pursue.
- **Watchdog and guard abilities:** High; he is a brave protector.
- **Ideal owner:** Strong leader, with time to train, exercise and groom; Bouviers love "calm attention."
- **Ideal home or environment:** House with fenced yard is a must. Don't let him "run free." Bouviers prefer to be outside, where they can run and play, but not exiled from the house; a dog-door with access from the house to the fenced yard is ideal; he does best in the country, but also adapts to suburban and even city living.
- **Behavioral problems:** Possibly controlling nature and passive resistance.
- **Health problems:** Possibly problems with hip dysplasia and bloat (gastric torsion), as well as other hereditary issues.
- **Recommendations:** Don't buy a Bouvier because of appearance; Bouviers need leadership and early obedience training because they may become dominant; they require much grooming and care; they can be expensive to maintain.

Do You Know about Hip Dysplasia?

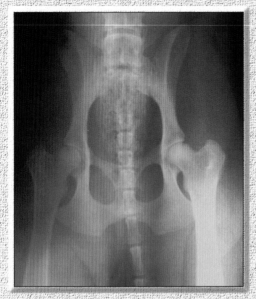

X-ray of a dog with "Good" hips.

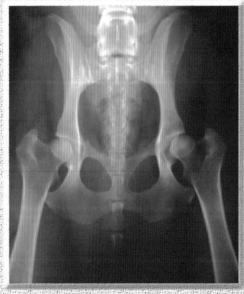

X-ray of a dog with "Moderate" dysplastic hips.

Hip dysplasia is a fairly common condition found in pure-bred dogs. When a dog has hip dysplasia, his hind leg has an incorrectly formed hip joint. By constant use of the hip joint, it becomes more and more loose, wears abnormally and may become arthritic.

Hip dysplasia can only be confirmed with an x-ray, but certain symptoms may indicate a problem. Your dog may have a hip dysplasia problem if he walks in a peculiar manner, hops instead of smoothly runs, uses his hind legs in unison (to keep the pressure off the weak joint), has trouble getting up from a prone position or always sits with both legs together on one side of his body.

As the dog matures, he may adapt well to life with a bad hip, but in a few years the arthritis develops and many dogs with hip dysplasia become crippled.

Hip dysplasia is considered an inherited disease and only can be diagnosed definitively by x-ray when the dog is two years old, although symptoms often appear earlier. Some experts claim that a special diet might help your puppy outgrow the bad hip, but the usual treatments are surgical. The removal of the pectineus muscle, the removal of the round part of the femur, reconstructing the pelvis and replacing the hip with an artificial one are all surgical interventions that are expensive, but they are usually very successful. Follow the advice of your veterinarian.

exceptionally strong working dog with great stamina and endurance. The combination of his personality traits and physical characteristics makes him able, with adequate training, to excel in many areas of competition and

Qjuero von Gewdraa Oel, practicing the protection work of the Belgian-CQN program. The men in the bite suits are referred to as "criminals" or "apaches." Photos courtesy of *Woef.*

dog sport, such as obedience training, agility, carting, conformation showing, guard or defense programs, tracking, herding, etc. He is excellent as a police or service dog and does very well in various activities that require special training.

The Bouvier des Flandres is very successful in the sport of Schutzhund (which means "defense dog"), or, in his native regions, in the International Working Regulations program IPO (the *Internationale Prüfungs-sordnung*), which is the slightly different international form of Schutzhund. In some countries (such as the Netherlands), he participates in police trials and the so-called "ring sport" (of Belgium and France). However, these disciplines include not only obedience and tracking but also protection or defense work, and thus are controversial in most English-speaking countries because, during the defense exercises, the dogs are taught to attack the "criminal" or "agitator" (which is a defense-work assistant in complete defense outfit, with padded armguard and soft stick).

A Bouvier is always willing to work but he is also very playful. Yet he differs from other working breeds in his more serene, calm and thoughtful nature. While excitable behavior is seen in many breeds, including other working and herding breeds, the Bouvier distinguishes himself by his low level of irritability or excitability. His nature is more quiet and placid than that of other herding dogs and most of the working breeds.

Although always ready for action when necessary, the Bouvier is not impetuous. For example, he will first wait to see which way the cat jumps. For this reason, some trainers find him rather slow to take action. However, this trait also constitutes a great advantage, because it allows the Bouvier owner to better avoid a possibly dangerous situation by tempering his dog before the dog's excitement becomes uncontrollable. So, because of his laid-back disposition, a Bouvier is more amenable to control than many other working breeds.

The drawbacks of the Bouvier's character are related to its being too strong in many individuals, a character that is stable and very self-confident, rather independent and stubborn and sometimes dominant or even aggressive. The Bouvier can sometimes growl, bark threateningly or exhibit other aggressive behavior, but this is directed mostly toward cats and other small animals. Aggressive behavior may be exhibited to a lesser degree toward other dogs and strangers, and much more rarely toward family members. Nevertheless, a Bouvier may resist control or

Randa van 't Hof ter Windeke, training for the protection phase of Schutzhund work.

Hosey Dukke Bianca fan it Hanenheim, Bundessieger 1981, Dutch Champion 1983.

domination and, as a consequence, he needs strong leadership from his owner.

Barking is a natural reaction of a watchful dog. A watchdog barks to alert his owners and to guard his family, property, home, car, etc. However, when your puppy barks for hours when left alone in the house, the reason behind it is loneliness, which is more appropriately labeled separation anxiety. Excessive barking can and must be stopped through appropriate training, but is not a behavioral problem in Bouviers.

As to the character and temperament, great individual differences are possible, even within the same breed. Bouviers are, in general, rather serene and pensive. If your Bouvier shows excitable behavior, you can correct it by always trying to remain calm and quiet, by enabling the dog to expend energy with plenty of exercise and by avoiding any activities that trigger excitable behavior.

ACTIVITIES AND TRAINING

If you are an experienced dog trainer and you acquire a Bouvier, it goes without saying that you are making an excellent choice. We know that today only a few

Bouviers are used for their original task—herding or cattle droving—but they surely are among the most "multi-talented" of all breeds. As mentioned, Bouviers can be trained to high levels of achievement in all kinds of competitive disciplines, such as obedience, tracking, ring sport and defense programs, and all kinds of working trials, performance tests and related activities.

Besides training disciplines and sports, conformation shows also have become increasingly popular with Bouvier owners. However, if you want to show, you must realize that your dog can only be successful if he is in good condition and if he displays the breed's desired physical and mental characteristics to a high degree. Taking part in a dog show can be exciting but, when your dog does not fare well, it can be deeply disillusioning. Showing is not a sport for everyone, and a new owner must decide whether or not he intends to show before purchasing his puppy. A breeder who knows that you intend to show will sell you a puppy with "show potential," one that the breeder feels will be conformationally correct. Frequently, puppies have minor faults that, while not affecting their ability to be ideal pets, render them less desirable for the show ring.

Many owners become interested in showing their Bouviers des Flandres. This is only natural because, when you have a beautiful Bouvier, you rightly feel proud and want to display this enthusiasm publicly. No specialized skills are required to show your dog, but the dog must be in good condition, possess a well-kept and well-groomed coat and not be shy, aggressive or nervous. When showing a Bouvier, never underestimate the importance of the coat, which has to be perfectly groomed. Grooming the pet Bouvier already requires time, regularity and expertise, but show grooming requires a great deal of nearly professional skill, aside from being time-consuming and

Part of the "fun" of grooming a Bouvier is getting him up on the grooming table. Hopefully this task is easier than it looks!

HEALTH CONCERNS IN THE BOUVIER

Increased attention to research has brought numerous health issues to light in the Bouvier breed. With this knowledge and continued research, breeders can concentrate on careful selective breeding to minimize and eventually eliminate those disorders with hereditary bases. Although the Bouvier is a robust, healthy breed overall, breeders and owners must be aware of potential health concerns. None of these conditions is exclusive to the Bouvier, but the way a disease is inherited as well as the frequency with which it occurs can vary from breed to breed. The Bouvier Health Foundation (www.bouvierhealthfoundation.org) was formed to distribute information and raise funds for health research. The foundation works closely with the health committee of the ABdFC (www.bouvier.org). The following list provides simple descriptions of possible health concerns in the breed. Visit the foundation's and club's websites for a more complete list and more detailed information.

Eye problems: Glaucoma is the main eye disease seen in the breed; increased pressure in the eye causes pain and can progress to blindness. Also seen are cataracts (opacity in the eye), ectropion and entropion (lid abnormalities), microphthalmia (eyeball developmental disorder, possibly causing blindness), persistent pupillary membranes (failure of blood vessels to regress normally, interfering with vision) and persistent hyperplastic primary vitreous (presence of membrane over eye; in the Bouvier, associated with other problems and can lead to cataracts, glaucoma and blindness if not removed).

Orthopedic problems: Hip dysplasia: Ball-and-socket joint of hip do not fit together properly, causing pain and lameness. Can be diagnosed by x-ray at two years of age and managed therapeutically, medically or surgically, depending on severity. Elbow dysplasia: Refers to a complex of disorders causing pain and lameness in the elbow, among them osteochondritis. Also can be diagnosed by x-ray at two years old.

Bloat (gastric dilatation/torsion): A life-threatening condition seen most frequently in large deep-chested breeds. The stomach twists on itself and fills with air, blocking exit points and causing bloating and shock. A dog can die if not treated by a vet immediately at the first sign of any symptom (discussed in more detail in feeding section of this book).

Thyroid dysfunction/hypothyroidism: Autoimmune disorder in which immune system destroys thyroid gland, resulting in deficient metabolism. All dogs should be tested regularly, as age of onset can vary. Treatment is available to help affected dogs live normal lives.

Subaortic stenosis: A major concern in the breed; research being conducted to find the genetic marker. Narrowing of aorta and obstruction impede blood flow, putting added stress on the heart. Usually diagnosed in young pups, detected by heart murmur. Testing is essential, as symptoms are often not evident in milder cases, yet dogs can die suddenly if the condition is undetected and untreated.

Cancer: A major killer of all types of dog. Lymphoma is a major concern in the Bouvier, although the breed can be affected by any of various types of cancers. As in humans, early detection is the key to treatment. Changes in behavior, appetite, bathroom habits or exercise habits and changes to the body (lumps, weakness, sores, etc.) all can be symptoms and warrant veterinary attention.

Bouvier des Flandres myopathy: A paddling gait that results from muscle weakness and atrophy; difficulty swallowing and regurgitating/megaesophagus are common in affected dogs. This condition occurs mainly in young dogs (two years old or younger).

Skin problems: Atopic dermatitis refers to patches of itchy skin caused by autoimmune response to allergens; alopecic syndrome refers to hair loss due to various causes.

Mouth problems: A cleft palate (where mouth plates fail to close) and/or cleft lip (fissure in upper lip) cause food/liquid to enter airways. An elongated soft palate can partially block airways and impede breathing. Overshot/undershot jaws can cause eating difficulties depending on severity.

Hernia: Hiatal hernia: The hiatus at the bottom of the esophagus does not function properly in keeping abdominal contents down. Symptoms include vomiting, excessive salivation; can be controlled through diet and possibly surgery. Umbilical hernia: A piece of skin, organ or fat protrudes through incompletely closed umbilical ring. Can correct on its own or be treated surgically. These two types of hernia are unrelated.

Deafness: Present in young puppies; testing is available to confirm hearing or deafness in one or both ears.

Ectopic ureters: Malformation of ureters, causing urine dribbling, possible incontinence and, in females, vaginitis.

Epilepsy: Brain disorder that causes seizures; the disorder usually becomes evident in dogs under one year of age. Can be controlled through medication and avoidance of certain drugs. Seizures may be symptomatic of thyroid problems; any dog with seizures should be tested for thyroid function.

Megaesophagus: Esophagus fails to force food into stomach, causing regurgitation. Other symptoms include muscle weakness and atrophy, dry nose and mucous membranes, breathing disorders and diarrhea.

Hermaphrodite: Full male and female chromosomes present in a dog of either sex. Evident in young pups; symptoms include malformation of sex organs, abnormal urination, infertility.

Inflammatory bowel disease: Gastrointestinal disorder that is not curable, but controllable. Sometimes can be caused by dietary factors. Symptoms include weight loss, vomiting, diarrhea or other bowel-movement abnormalities. Dogs must be tested to confirm IBD.

Laryngeal paralysis: Obstruction of airflow due to nerve problems, paralyzing muscles of larynx. Symptoms include wheezing, difficult breathing, exercise intolerance and difference in sound of bark. Males are affected more frequently than females. Surgical treatment is recommended.

Portosystemic shunt: Presence of extra blood vessel(s), allowing blood to bypass liver. Can be diagnosed by x-ray and treated surgically. Symptoms usually evident in dogs under one year of age.

expensive. A Bouvier never can be successfully shown without the coat in top condition.

Training is of paramount importance, because judges will not tolerate unruly exhibits. Visit a dog show to learn the protocol and meet the exhibitors. Before entering your dog, you are well advised to train him for the show ring, so as to teach him proper ring manners. If you are to handle your dog yourself, you also will need to learn the rules and procedures. You also should study the breed standard of the Bouvier des Flandres so that you will understand what the judges are looking for in a "perfect specimen." A handling class to introduce the owner and dog to the showing procedure can make a world of difference for the novice showman.

CONSIDERATIONS FOR THE PET BOUVIER OWNER

If you are not interested in showing, advanced training, trials, etc., the Bouvier des Flandres is still an excellent choice for a pet and family dog. In fact, the great majority of Bouviers are kept simply as pets, as the breed certainly offers many delightful qualities to owners. However, it cannot be stressed enough that with the pet dog, especially one with a strong personality and independence of mind such as the Bouvier, basic training is not optional! Rather, it is an

"absolute must" to make him a suitable home companion. If left to grow up without guidance from you, your Bouvier will make his own rules.

Some of the well-known qualities that make the Bouvier des Flandres a wonderful companion and family member are:

- Sound health and low incidence of medical problems (the explanations of potential problems are intended to inform, but their occurrence is low).
- Loyal dedication to his family.
- If properly educated, responds well to commands and complies with house rules.
- Innate propensity to protect and guard your home and property.

However, no matter how many wonderful qualities the breed

Bouviers adapt well to many disciplines, and dog shows have become increasingly popular with Bouvier owners in recent years.

possesses, a potential owner must also consider the following before purchasing a Bouvier:

- He does not shed, but the amount of required grooming is considerable.
- He needs human companionship and he doesn't like to be left alone.
- Early socialization is a must—this means that the puppy has to be exposed to as many different people and situations as possible.
- He doesn't always show his affection outwardly; he tends to be aloof.
- He is an efficient transporter of dirt and mud; his beard retains particles of food, collects water and can leave a wet trail across your floors, so you may have to live with a little bit of mess in your home.
- His body odor can be unpleasant and he is said to be one of the more flatulent breeds.
- He needs physical activity, which will make him an excellent playmate and an ideal companion when you walk or train him. It is a must for you to provide him with daily exercise, as a Bouvier may be rather lazy and not disposed to exercise on his own in your fenced yard.

It has to be made very clear that the Bouvier's impressive appearance, especially in the show ring, is the result of many hours of professional grooming.

As a matter of fact, his natural look is that of a shaggy farm dog, with dirt clinging to his coat. One must realize that his true beauty lies in his personality.

Bouviers have the reputation of being good family dogs. They become deeply attached to their families. They are good guardians that do not need to be trained to bite or attack on command in order to be effective; rather, they are guardians of the "dissuasive" type. Their size and air of calm appraisal can be very intimidating. Their dark coat color and their sturdy, shaggy, almost bestial appearance have such a deterrent effect that aspiring intruders or burglars quickly decide to clear out and to look for "easier" victims.

Bouviers are great with children, who of course must be taught how to behave with them; otherwise, serious problems can occur. Too often it happens that the Bouvier is given a bad reputation. You may have heard that he is ferocious and that he becomes ornery as he ages, and still other slander of this kind. You will always find, however, that such false remarks come from people who have never owned a Bouvier. On the contrary, I very often hear that people who have owned Bouviers cannot get used to another breed. Under the rough bark of this rugged cattle driver is hidden a golden heart.

Nothing seems to escape the Bouvier's beard... a little bit of mess is a fact of life for Bouvier owners!

Bouviers are friendly, even-tempered dogs who are not always overly demonstrative but like to show affection to those they hold dear.

During my 50 years of involvement in canine sports, I have never heard of a Bouvier des Flandres who has bitten a child or his master.

Bouviers are intelligent, adaptable and protective. All of these attributes ensure their continued progress and increasing popularity for showing, participation in many canine sports, specialized training or working, and, of course, for selection as dedicated and beautiful pets. The breed rightly has acquired an enviable reputation for balanced temperament and strength of character, forged through many generations of use as working dogs. More important than his obedience, intellect and service to man is the Bouvier's legendary loyalty. When you give him the proper education, care and love, your Bouvier will give you the devotion, the discreet but immense love and the unconditional fidelity that have made him famous throughout the world.

In 1982, on the occasion of the centenary anniversary of the Société Royale Saint-Hubert, Justin Chastel, the architect and the founder of the modern Bouvier des Flandres, wrote what follows in an article on his beloved breed: "We think that, in spite of the diffusion of the Bouvier des Flandres all over the world, the breed is not always rated at its true value."

HEART-HEALTHY
In this modern age of ever-improving cardio-care, no doctor or scientist can dispute the advantages of owning a dog to lower a person's risk of heart disease. Studies have proven that petting a dog, walking a dog and grooming a dog all show positive results toward lowering your blood pressure. The simple routine of exercising your dog—going outside with the dog and walking, jogging or playing catch—is heart-healthy in and of itself. If you are normally less active than your physician thinks you should be, adopting a dog may be a smart option to improve your own quality of life as well as that of another creature.

BOUVIER DES FLANDRES

Farley Madame v.d. Duca Vallei, pictured here winning Best of Breed at an American show, is an American, Dutch, German and Luxembourg champion.

Bouvier, you can read the breed standard. However, for the novice who has not yet acquired sufficient knowledge of canine structure and terminology, the breed standard in itself is not an adequate guide.

A breed standard is used by the governing kennel clubs to describe the ideal or "model" dog of each recognized breed. Show dogs are judged against this standard, which describes the desired physical and temperamental characteristics of the perfect specimen. Breed standards for each breed are put into a common format and points of the dog are organized in a similar order, such as the judge would view the dog in the ring. He first evaluates the general

Every owner of a Bouvier des Flandres one day asks himself the question, "What does the perfect Bouvier look like?" or "How good is my dog as a representative of his breed?" Of course, everyone wants to believe that his dog is "quite close to perfection." To determine the quality of your

appearance and breed-specific characteristics, and then the dog's temperament. Next, he judges the morphology (form and structure) or conformation of the dog from front to rear, starting with head and skull and ending with the tail. Eventually, the dog has to move so that the judge can assess movement and gait. FCI standards, for example, end by listing faults, the most important (and worst) being the disqualifying faults. American Kennel Club standards, however, may mention faults either at the end or within each section, sometimes ending the entire standard with a summary of faults.

As to the general appearance, the silhouette and the proportions of dogs, three types can be distinguished. Dogs can be "longilineal," or "long-lined," which means slender and fine, having a long skull and fit for the race. Sighthounds are examples of this type. The second type is "brevilineal," or "short-lined," which means stocky, compact and robust, having a rather short skull, and fit for guard work and for pulling. The third type is "intermediate," or "mediolineal," which is how the majority of breeds are defined. Shepherd dogs are examples of this type.

Sometimes we read that the Bouvier is "brevilineal" (short-lined), which in fact is an exaggeration. The Bouvier, from a morphological point of view, is rather "sub-brevilineal," meaning

that he falls between the classifications of mediolineal and brevilineal. These terms and definitions are important, because the differences between shepherd dogs and cattle dogs relate much more to form and structure than to their working capacities or use in competition training (obedience, tracking, protection, police or service work). It means, in essence, that Bouviers generally are much more powerfully built than shepherd dogs.

The "type," meaning the general outline or appearance, of most breeds has changed dramatically since their origins or since their official recognition, or even since World War II. To a certain degree, this is also the case with the Bouvier des Flandres. When most people consider what a "dog" looks like, they often picture one that is lupine, or wolf-like, in appearance, one that generally resembles a shepherd dog in type. Consequently, in order to understand what a Bouvier truly should look like, it

Dutch and International Champion Spencer Jordina v.d. Boevers Garden, IPO III.

Ike Pepper van
de Duca Vallei,
European Youth
Champion, an
example of a
top-quality
natural-eared
European dog.

should be helpful to list the important features of the breed that distinguish him from most of the shepherd dog breeds:

- A heavier skeleton, stronger legs and a more robust or sturdy appearance.
- The impression of massiveness of the head; the length of muzzle (from nose to stop), which is shorter than the length of skull (from stop to occiput).
- A square body, which means that the length from the front of the chest to the back of the buttocks is equal to the height at the withers.
- The well-sprung (but not cylindrical) ribs, which means that the chest is broad and that flat ribs are a serious fault.
- The angulation (the angles formed at the joints, where the bones meet), which is not excessive; rather, it is moderate to normal, so that the hind legs are well under the body when the dog is standing or in "show stance."

When comparing the American Kennel Club's standard for the Bouvier des Flandres to those of the FCI and The Kennel Club of England, no significant differences can be seen, except in some specifications such as the height at the withers and the prescribed bite (position of the upper and the lower front teeth when the jaws are closed). According to the FCI and The Kennel Club standards, which list measurements in metric terms, the height is 62–68 cm (approximately 24.5–27 inches) for dogs and 59–65 cm (approximately 23–25.5 inches) for bitches; in the AKC standard, however, the maximum limit is higher for both sexes (27.5 inches in dogs; 26.5 inches in bitches), which surely is a bit of a difference. As to the bite, the American and British standards only permit a scissors bite; according to the FCI standard, scissors and pincer bites are both accepted.

In the Bouvier, as in most other breeds, some faults are considered serious or even disqualifying in the show ring. Serious faults in the Bouvier include rangy dogs, narrow muzzles, flat ribs, sloping croups, light eyes and silky or woolly coats. Disqualifying faults are shyness or aggressiveness, an atypical appearance, too many missing teeth, over- or undershot mouths, turning inward or outward of the eyelids (entropion or ectropion, respectively) and only one testicle (monorchidism) or neither testicle (cryptorchidism) descended into the scrotum. Colors also can be disqualifying, such as a coat that is chocolate brown or has too much white, or a nose that is not black.

Taking all of the standards into consideration, a summary of the characteristics of the Bouvier des Flandres could read as follows:

American and Canadian Champion Deewal Quinn.

Powerfully built, without heaviness; head appearing massive, with beard and mustache giving forbidding expression; proportion of skull to muzzle 3 to 2; nose always black; eyes slightly oval, as dark as possible; ears upstanding and set on high, carried erect; when not cropped, ears in proportion to head and hanging flat to side of head; scissor or pincer bite; neck strong and well muscled; compact, square, short-coupled body; deep and broad chest, ribs well sprung; withers slightly marked; back and loins short, muscled, without weakness; horizontal croup; belly only slightly tucked up; tail docked to two-thirds vertebrae, or, when natural, carried under horizontal, in action held higher, but not curled or not over back; forelegs strong and absolutely straight, pasterns sloping very slightly; hindquarters powerful, strongly muscled; feet round and compact, nails black; coat abundant, hair coarse to touch, slightly tousled, about 6 cm (about 2.5 inches) long; upper lip with mustache, lower lip with beard, and eyebrows formed of upright hairs; coat color mostly gray, brindle or with black overlay; wholly black coat also allowed, but not favored; nose, lips and eyelids always strongly pigmented.

It is important for the preservation of the breed and its international esteem that there be a unified type all over the world. During the last decades, there has been a slow evolution toward what is now considered better type; namely, a more developed and slightly more angulated wrist, a deeper underline (brisket and belly), a firmer back and loins and a horizontal croup. This evolution has greatly improved the silhouette of the Bouvier. Nevertheless, too many Bouviers that are too long in body are still seen. This is rather surprising, because in the three standards we can read that the body is square, the length being equal to the height.

We have also to mention that, over the last decades, an evolution in type and characteristics has taken place that really has been harmful to the aptitudes of the Bouvier as a working breed. First case in point: in many countries, the Bouviers have become too big and too heavy. Working dogs should be strong, energetic and very active, but also quick and agile. When these qualities can be found in dogs that are watchful, intelligent and trainable, all of the requirements for a perfect, versatile working dog are met. However, Bouviers that are oversized and/or too heavy will lack the necessary energy, endurance and agility.

A second regrettable evolution concerns the coat texture or quality. The outer hairs should be rough, harsh, dry and coarse to the touch. The Bouvier's coat should protect him in all weather and enable him to perform the most arduous tasks. All too often, coats are seen today that are more abundant and, we have to admit, more attractive than those of former days; on the other hand, they are much softer than coats of proper texture for working dogs. These days, the majority of the modern, even successful, Bouviers have coats that are heavier and softer than allowed according to the standard. Apparently, the show look and fashion trends have "won" over the working-dog look and, therefore, the breed standard.

Another concern about the evolution in type is related to the "angulation" and, thus, the gait or movement. Movement is one of the most important considerations in evaluating dogs. Unfortunately, in most standards, including that of the Bouvier, the description of the desired movement is somewhat incomplete. Nothing is said about the stride, which is the distance covered by each foot in the process of a single step. It is evident that the movement should be free and easy. When viewed from the side, we should see a strong rear drive, which is transmitted through a firm loin and back to the forequarters. However, when Bouviers of the "modern type" are trotting, the movement very often covers too much ground, which means that the distance covered by each stride is too great. Such an "extended trot" is not typical for a powerfully and squarely built dog such as the Bouvier, although, in the show ring, it has an eye-catching appeal. Nonetheless, an exaggerated stride such as this is usually the result of over-angulation of fore- and hindquarters.

"Angulation" refers to the angles formed in the fore- and hindquarters at the joints by the meeting of the bones. The Bouvier's angulation is said to be "normal"; accordingly, the reach of stride and extension also will be moderate to normal. From this normal angulation comes a very important feature of the desired general appearance of the Bouvier; namely, that its strong and sturdy hind legs, when standing or in "show stance," are placed "under the body." The Bouvier's legs should not be, as in the German Shepherd, in a backward-slanting position (referred to as *Rückständig* in German). This position is typical for breeds having a long "second thigh," which is the part of the hind leg between the stifle and the hock joint. Generally, one doesn't realize that animals that are strongly angulated in the hindquarters have less standing power or standing ability (*Stehvermögen* in German), which means that they lack the strength or endurance to stand for a long time without sitting or lying down.

Finally, we need to mention a possible divergence of type in two different Bouviers; namely, working Bouviers and show Bouviers. It would be very unfavorable if this divergence has already progressed so far that going back to only one type—the original type, a versatile working dog that was bred for one purpose, would no longer be possible. If the original creators and promoters of the breed could see today's shows and observe the grooming areas where the Bouviers are trimmed (or "over-trimmed"), brushed, quaffed, etc., they would "turn over in their graves." We know that a Bouvier des Flandres has to be well trimmed in order to be shown, and that this requires a lot of practice, thorough knowledge of the breed and a very clear picture of a good Bouvier on the groomer's part. However, over-grooming to prepare a Bouvier for a show, with the intention of enhancing the qualities of the dog, as well as hiding its inadequacies, is not well received by many breed fanciers. Excessive grooming offends people who still believe that the serene, rustic nature and the natural rugged appearance of this farmer's dog absolutely have to be preserved. Furthermore, they believe that a Bouvier that no longer possesses the ability of an all-purpose working dog is not a real Bouvier.

THE AMERICAN KENNEL CLUB STANDARD FOR THE BOUVIER DES FLANDRES

General Appearance: The Bouvier des Flandres is a powerfully built, compact, short-coupled, rough-coated dog of notably rugged appearance. He gives the impression of great strength without any sign of heaviness or clumsiness in his overall makeup. He is agile, spirited and bold, yet his serene, well behaved disposition denotes his steady, resolute and fearless character. His gaze is alert and brilliant, depicting his intelligence, vigor and daring. By nature he is an equable dog. His origin is that of a cattle herder and general farmer's helper, including cart pulling. He is an ideal farm dog. His harsh double coat protects him in all weather, enabling him to perform the most arduous tasks. He has been used as an ambulance and messenger dog. Modern times find him as a watch and guard dog as well as a family friend, guardian and protector. His physical and mental characteristics and deportment, coupled with his olfactory abilities, his intelligence and initiative enable him to also perform as a tracking dog and a guide dog for the blind. The following description is that of the ideal Bouvier des Flandres. Any deviation from this is to be penalized to the extent of the deviation.

Size, Proportion, Substance: *Size*—The height as measured at the withers: Dogs, from 24.5 to 27.5 inches; bitches, from 23.5 to 26.5 inches. In each sex, the ideal height is the median of the two limits, i.e., 26 inches for a dog and 25 inches for a bitch. Any dog or bitch deviating from the minimum or maximum limits mentioned shall be severely penalized. *Proportion*—The *length* from the point of the shoulder to the tip of the buttocks is equal to the height from the ground to the highest point of the withers. A long-bodied dog should be seriously faulted. *Substance*—Powerfully built, strong boned, well muscled, without any sign of heaviness or clumsiness.

Head: The head is impressive in scale, accentuated by beard and

This figurine shows clearly, although somewhat excessively, the desired physical appearance of the Bouvier.

Correct head with cropped ears.

mustache. It is in proportion to body and build. The *expression* is bold and alert. *Eyes* neither protrude nor are sunken in the sockets. Their shape is oval with the axis on the horizontal plane, when viewed from the front. Their color is a dark brown. The eye rims are black without lack of pigment and the haw is barely visible. Yellow or light eyes are to be strongly penalized, along with a walleyed or staring expression. *Ears* placed high and alert. If cropped, they are to be a triangular contour and in proportion to the size of the head. The inner corner of the ear should be in line with the outer corner of the eye. Ears that are too low or too closely set are serious faults. *Skull*

well developed and flat, slightly less wide than long. When viewed from the side, the top lines of the skull and the muzzle are parallel. It is wide between the ears, with the frontal groove barely marked. The *stop* is more apparent than real, due to upstanding eyebrows. The proportions of length of skull to length of muzzle are 3 to 2. *Muzzle* broad, strong, well filled out, tapering gradually toward the nose without ever becoming snipy or pointed. A narrow, snipy muzzle is faulty. *Nose* large, black, well developed, round at the edges, with flared nostrils. A brown, pink or spotted nose is a serious fault. The cheeks are flat and lean, with the lips being dry and tight fitting. The jaws are powerful and of equal length. The teeth are strong, white and healthy, with the incisors meeting in a scissors bite. Overshot or undershot bites are to be severely penalized.

Neck, Topline, and Body: The *neck* is strong and muscular, widening gradually into the shoulders. When viewed from the side, it is gracefully arched with proud carriage. A short, squatty neck is faulty. No dewlap. *Back* short, broad, well muscled with firm level topline. It is supple and flexible with no sign of weakness. *Body* or *trunk* powerful, broad and short. The chest is broad, with the brisket extending to the elbow in depth. The ribs are deep and well sprung. The first ribs are slightly curved, the others well sprung and very well sloped nearing the rear, giving proper depth to the chest. Flat ribs or slabsidedness is to be strongly penalized. *Flanks* and *loins* short, wide and well muscled, without weakness. The abdomen is only slightly tucked up. The horizontal line of the back should mold unnoticeably into the curve of the rump, which is characteristically wide. A sunken or slanted croup is a serious fault. *Tail* is to be docked, leaving 2 or 3 vertebrae. It must be set high and align normally with the spinal column. Preferably carried upright in motion. Dogs born tailless should not be penalized.

Forequarters: Strong boned, well muscled and straight. The *shoulders* are relatively long, muscular but not loaded, with good layback. The shoulder blade and humerus are approximately the same length, forming an angle slightly greater than 90 degrees when standing. Steep shoulders are faulty. *Elbows* close to the body and parallel. Elbows which are too far out or in are faults. *Forearms* viewed either in profile or from the front are perfectly straight, parallel to each other and perpendicular to the ground. They are well muscled and strong boned. *Carpus* exactly in line

with the forearms. Strong boned. *Pasterns* quite short, slightly sloped. Dewclaws may be removed. Both forefeet and hind feet are rounded and compact, turning neither in nor out; the toes close and well arched; strong black nails; thick tough pads.

Hindquarters: Firm, well muscled with large, powerful hams. They should be parallel with the front legs when viewed from either front or rear. *Legs* moderately long, well muscled, neither too straight nor too inclined. *Thighs* wide and muscular. The upper thigh must be neither too straight nor too sloping. There is moderate angulation at the stifle. *Hocks* strong, rather close to the ground. When standing and seen from the rear, they will be straight and perfectly parallel to each other. In motion, they must turn neither in nor out. There is a slight angulation at the hock joint. Sickle or cowhocks are serious faults. *Metatarsi* hardy and lean, rather cylindrical and perpendicular to the ground when standing. If born with dewclaws, they are to be removed. *Feet* as in front.

Coat: A tousled, double coat capable of withstanding the hardest work in the most inclement weather. The outer hairs are rough and harsh, with the undercoat being fine, soft and dense. The coat may be trimmed slightly only

Correct head with natural ears of proper size and carriage.

the upper side of the muzzle. The upper lip with its heavy mustache and the chin with its heavy and rough beard give that gruff expression so characteristic of the breed. *Eyebrows*, erect hairs accentuating the shape of the eyes without ever veiling them.

Color: From fawn to black, passing through salt and pepper, gray and brindle. A small white star on the chest is allowed. Other than chocolate brown, white, or parti-color, which are to be severely penalized, no one color is to be favored.

Gait: The whole of the Bouvier des Flandres must be harmoniously proportioned to allow for a free, bold and proud gait. The reach of the forequarters must compensate for and be in balance with the driving power of the hindquarters. The back, while moving in a trot, will remain firm and flat. In general, the gait is the logical demonstration of the structure and build of the dog. It is to be noted that while moving at a fast trot, the properly built Bouvier will tend to single-track.

Temperament: The Bouvier is an equable dog, steady, resolute and fearless. Viciousness or shyness is undesirable.

Approved January 10, 2000
Effective Febraury 23, 2000

to accent the body line. Overtrimming which alters the natural rugged appearance is to be avoided. *Topcoat* must be harsh to the touch, dry, trimmed, if necessary, to a length of approximately 2.5 inches. A coat too long or too short is a fault, as is a silky or woolly coat. It is tousled without being curly. On the skull, it is short, and on the upper part of the back, it is particularly close and harsh always, however, remaining rough. *Ears* are rough-coated. *Undercoat* a dense mass of fine, close hair, thicker in winter. Together with the topcoat, it will form a water-resistant covering. A flat coat, denoting lack of undercoat is a serious fault. *Mustache* and *beard* very thick, with the hair being shorter and rougher on

Structural faults illustrated here include poor topline, long back, weak pasterns, Roman nose and straight rear. These faults are hidden by artful trimming, but will become apparent when the dog moves. Also, a judge will use his hands to feel under the coat for correct structure.

A correctly balanced and constructed Bouvier, distorted by improper trimming. He looks too straight in the rear and shows a bad topline. Since the coat tends to be heavier over the shoulders, rump and hips (cowboy chaps), these grooming errors are easy to commit. The coat is too long on the brisket and underbelly, making the dog appear too low on leg.

Bouvier with cropped ears and modern profuse, heavily trimmed coat.

Bouvier with natural ears and the more traditional tousled coat that is not as profuse.

This small bundle of fur will grow into a large, powerful working dog in almost no time... a major consideration that cannot be overlooked when choosing your breed.

BOUVIER DES FLANDRES

CONSIDER YOUR DECISION
Nothing is more exciting than selecting a Bouvier des Flandres puppy. When you and your family have decided that a Bouvier is really the most suitable dog for you, you can locate a recommended kennel and make a careful choice.

Before you talk to a breeder, you have to know what you intend to do with your new companion. Will you show your new Bouvier, or enter him in obedience or herding trials, or do

you simply desire a pet? Regardless, he must be part of your daily routine, now and in the years to come. The responsibilities you will have and the consequences of keeping a dog should be considered before you choose and visit a breeder, as your dog will rely completely on you.

The Bouvier is a wonderful dog, but you should only seriously begin your search for a puppy after considering the following:

- All of your family members should not only agree but also be enthusiastic about acquiring a Bouvier puppy.
- Your children should regard the

Puppies of top-quality breeding: Sato and Singa von Gewdraa Oel at eight weeks of age.

> **THE FAMILY TREE**
> Your puppy's pedigree is his family tree. Just as a child may resemble his parents and grandparents, so too will a puppy reflect the physical and temperamental qualities, good and bad, of his ancestors, especially those in the first two generations. Therefore it's important to know as much as possible about a puppy's immediate relatives. Reputable and experienced breeders should be able to explain the pedigree and why they chose to breed from the particular dogs they used.

dog as a playmate, not as a plaything, and should always be carefully supervised when interacting with the dog. Children

FINDING A QUALIFIED BREEDER

Before you begin your puppy search, ask for references from the breed club, your veterinarian and perhaps other breeders to refer you to someone they believe is reputable. Responsible breeders usually raise only one or two breeds of dog. Avoid any breeder who has several different breeds or has several litters at the same time. Dedicated breeders are usually involved with their breed club or another dog club. Many participate in some sport or activity related to their breed. Just as you want to be assured of the breeder's qualifications, the breeder wants to be assured that you will make a worthy owner. Expect the breeder to interview you, asking questions about your goals for the pup, your experience with dogs and what kind of home you will provide.

should be capable of respecting the dog, and they should be instructed in how to handle him properly.

- Taking care of a dog—feeding him, walking him, socializing and educating him, exercising him, grooming him (very important for a Bouvier, which will require weekly, sometimes daily grooming!), providing him with veterinary care and looking after him for a lifetime (10 to 12 years)—will be a time-consuming and long-term commitment.
- Food costs, veterinary bills, dog supplies, etc., must be included in the family budget.
- You should have a fenced yard or enclosure.
- When you go away on vacation, you must either take the dog with you or make arrangements for someone to look after him or somewhere to board him.

SELECTING AND ACQUIRING A PUPPY

If you are prepared to meet all of the requirements of dog ownership, you are ready to begin your search. You can start by researching reputable breeders and kennels, but do not act impulsively in your choice. Do not let your choice of a kennel be determined by its proximity to your home and do not buy the first puppy that licks your nose.

You can find advice on buying a Bouvier puppy from

people experienced in the breed. The best way to find a reputable breeder is to contact committee members of the national breed club, the American Bouvier des Flandres Club, who can refer you to reputable breeders. You may have to travel to meet the breeder, but you should be at least able to locate an ABdFC breeder in your county or state. A caring, responsible breeder raises his litters in his home. When showing you a litter, he will give you good advice and assistance. You can help the breeder by letting him know what you are looking for, such as the sex of puppy you prefer, and the purpose for which you desire the pup—as a family pet or for showing, breeding, training, working, etc. A good kennel consistently produces healthy and sound dogs, and also provides good after-sales service.

A responsible breeder will show you the mother of the litter and also the father, if he is available. The parents' appearance and behavior will give you some idea of your puppy's eventual appearance and temperament. The breeder will also explain to you how a pedigree is read and inform you about the litter's "bloodlines" (the direct ancestors in a pedigree), specifically the merits of the parents and grandparents. Do not underestimate the importance of the ancestors' character and

SELECTING FROM THE LITTER

Before you visit a litter of puppies, promise yourself that you won't fall for the first pretty face you see! Decide on your goals for your puppy—show prospect, working dog, obedience competitor, family companion—and then look for a puppy who displays the appropriate qualities. In most litters, there is an Alpha pup (the bossy puppy), and occasionally a shy fellow who is less confident, with the rest of the litter falling somewhere in the middle. "Middle-of-the-roaders" are safe bets for most families and novice competitors.

anatomical structure if you wish your puppy to grow up to be a high-quality adult Bouvier des Flandres. However, you need some luck, too. You have to realize that you are fortunate if a

Blake pup

puppy coming from "champion lines" becomes a champion; on the other hand, a champion that comes from inferior parents would be a miracle!

When you have chosen your breeder and go to visit a litter, watch the behavior of the puppies as they interact with each other. Do

PEDIGREE VS. REGISTRATION CERTIFICATE

Too often new owners are confused between these two important documents. Your puppy's pedigree, essentially a family tree, is a written record of a dog's genealogy of three generations or more. The pedigree will show you the names as well as performance titles of all dogs in your pup's background. Your breeder must provide you with a registration application, with his part properly filled out. You must complete the application and send it to the AKC with the proper fee. Every puppy must come from a litter that has been AKC-registered by the breeder, born in the US and from a sire and dam that are also registered with the AKC.

The seller must provide you with complete records to identify the puppy. The AKC requires that the seller provide the buyer with the following: breed; sex, color and markings; date of birth; litter number (when available); names and registration numbers of the parents; breeder's name; and date sold or delivered.

not choose a shy or retreating puppy, as he may grow to be insecure or fearful. On the other hand, very assertive puppies can develop into overly dominant adults. Try to select an outgoing, confident and alert puppy, one who looks healthy, is willing to play and comes running toward you. A puppy should not be fearful about noises. He should not hide but, rather, should show interest when you drop a metal object like a key or hit a metal pan with a spoon.

You should not buy any puppy of the litter, even one that seems to behave normally, if most of them show fear or cannot be approached. Ideally, when you enter a room with the litter, the pups should all approach you, jump on you and compete for attention. An extroverted character will be an advantage for training as well as showing. Take into consideration, though, that pups sleep as much as 18 hours a day and that your visit might coincide with one of their many naps.

It is rather difficult to make predictions about how a pup will develop and if his show potential will be realized, but an experienced breeder should be able to guide you in your choice of a potential show puppy, even as early as at eight weeks. There are very few experts in Bouviers, and even experts can be mistaken. Nonetheless, a good Bouvier puppy should have a substantial, firm and square body, with a well-sprung rib cage; a back or topline that already is firm and horizontal, with no dip behind the withers, no arched loins and no slope of the croup; legs, both front and rear, that are straight and parallel to each other, neither bowed nor placed too close together (no cowhock look from behind); and a head that should already be strong, with a muzzle, neither weak nor narrow, that is shorter than the skull. Choose a pup that, rather than hopping, already is able to trot easily, with a parallel movement of the fore- and the hindquarters; the topline should remain firm and level during movement.

The coat texture, coat color and pigmentation are important in the Bouvier des Flandres. The puppy's hair should already tend to feel harsh or crisp. The intensity or darkness of the coat color should be at least medium gray. Don't buy a pup with fawn, pale or washed-out coloration. Any white should be avoided, except a small patch on the forechest. Pigmentation, in canine language, refers to the color of the nose, lips, gums (which in the Bouvier

A SHOW PUPPY

If you plan to show your puppy, you must first deal with a reputable breeder who shows his dogs and has had some success in the conformation ring. The puppy's pedigree should include one or more champions in the first and second generation. You should be familiar with the breed and breed standard so you can know what qualities to look for in your puppy. The breeder's observations and recommendations also are invaluable aids in selecting your future champion. If you consider an older puppy, be sure that the puppy has been properly socialized with people and animals and not isolated in a kennel with only limited exposure to the goings-on in the household.

GETTING ACQUAINTED

When visiting a litter, ask the breeder for suggestions on how best to interact with the puppies. If possible, get right into the middle of the pack and sit down with them. Observe which pups climb into your lap and which ones shy away. Toss a toy for them to chase and bring back to you. It's easy to fall in love with the puppy who picks you, but keep your future objectives in mind before you make your final decision.

is dark or black, except the nose, which *must* be black) and eyelids (which should be black-rimmed).

Decide which sex you prefer. There are some specific differences. Males are certainly physically more impressive. They also have a greater tendency to be independent and to wander farther afield. They are more pugnacious and sometimes aggressive toward other males. They mark their territory in a demonstrative manner. Bitches are more feminine, smaller and less powerfully built. Unspayed females normally come into season once every 6 months for 21 days. At the beginning, the heat cycle is marked with a clear mucus-like discharge from the vagina. Very often, however, the bitch's frequent licking is noticed first. After about seven days, the discharge is bloody and can be copious; during the third week, the discharge eases up. During the bitch's season, you will have to keep her away from male dogs in order to prevent unwanted matings. Bitches are generally more friendly, a little more affectionate and more submissive. Moreover, some people find that a bitch is easier to house-train than a male. Nevertheless, none of these sex differences should be overemphasized. In fact, both sexes are highly trainable and remarkably dedicated to their owners, and many sex-related issues are eliminated or diminished by neutering/spaying, which the breeder likely will require for pups not destined for showing or breeding.

The best age to bring a puppy home is between seven and eight weeks, certainly not older than nine weeks. The reason is that during the so-called socialization period (8 to 12 weeks), the pups should be handled by a wide variety of people, exposed to as many experiences as possible and have contact with other dogs, other animals and humans, without becoming stressed. Early socialization begins with the breeder, but it is the new owner's responsibility to continue socializing the pup after taking him home. Pups that remain with the breeder for too long miss out on the crucial socialization experiences of the "outside world" at the prime age.

You should ask the breeder to show you the parents' registration documents, certificates of titles and performance (shows, temperament tests, obedience and herding trials, etc.) and health certificates. Ask the breeder whether the pups have been wormed, inoculated, etc., and obtain the necessary documentation. Be certain that your chosen puppy looks healthy; a potbelly is a possible sign of worms.

When you have made your purchase, a responsible and caring breeder will also give you a diet sheet and possibly some food for pup's first meals in his new home. Like many purchasers, you will have questions as your puppy grows up. You can keep in touch with the breeder for many years to come, as a good breeder will be willing to give you advice throughout your Bouvier's life. Choose a breeder with whom you feel comfortable, but don't trouble him about insignificant problems.

A COMMITTED NEW OWNER

By now you should understand what makes the Bouvier des Flandres a most unique and special dog, one that may fit nicely into your family and lifestyle. If you have researched breeders, you should be able to recognize a knowledgeable and responsible Bouvier des Flandres breeder who cares not only about his pups but also about what kind of owner you will be. If you have completed the final step in your new journey, you have found a litter, or possibly two, of quality Bouvier des Flandres pups.

A visit with the puppies and their breeder is an education in itself. Breed research, breeder selection and puppy visitation are very important aspects of finding

At seven weeks of age, this pup is just about ready to leave the breeder for his new home.

SIGNS OF A HEALTHY PUPPY

Healthy puppies are robust little fellows who are alert and active, sporting shiny coats and supple skin. They should not appear lethargic, bloated or pot-bellied, nor should they have flaky skin or runny or crusted eyes or noses. Their stools should be firm and well formed, with no evidence of blood or mucus.

iors indicate about each pup's temperament. Which type of pup will complement your family dynamics is best determined by observing the puppies in action within their "pack." Your breeder's expertise and recommendations are so valuable. Although you may fall in love with a bold and brassy male, the breeder may suggest that another pup would be best for you. The breeder's experience in rearing Bouvier des Flandres pups and matching their temperaments with appropriate humans offers the best assurance that your pup will meet your needs and expectations.

We can't overemphasize the fact that the decision to live with a Bouvier des Flandres is a serious commitment and not one to be taken lightly. This puppy is a living sentient being that will be dependent on you for basic survival for his entire life. Beyond the basics of survival—food, water, shelter and protection—he needs much, much more. The new pup needs love, nurturing and a proper canine education to mold him into a responsible, well-behaved canine citizen. Your Bouvier des Flandres's health and good manners will need consistent monitoring and regular "tune-ups," so your job as a responsible dog owner will be ongoing throughout every stage of his life. If you are not prepared to accept these responsibilities and commit

the puppy of your dreams. Beyond that, these things also lay the foundation for a successful future with your pup. By spending time with the puppies, you will be able to recognize certain behaviors and what these behav-

COST OF OWNERSHIP

The purchase price of your puppy is merely the first expense in the typical dog budget. Quality dog food, veterinary care (sickness and health maintenance), dog supplies and grooming costs will add up to big bucks every year. Can you adequately afford to support a canine addition to the family?

to them for the next decade, likely longer, then you are not prepared to own a dog of any breed.

Although the responsibilities of owning a dog may at times tax your patience, the joy of living with your Bouvier des Flandres far outweighs the workload, and a well-mannered adult dog is worth your time and effort. Before your very eyes, your pup will grow up to be your most loyal friend, devoted to you unconditionally.

YOUR BOUVIER DES FLANDRES SHOPPING LIST

Just as expectant parents prepare a nursery for their baby, so should you ready your home for the arrival of your Bouvier des Flandres pup. If you have the necessary puppy supplies purchased and in place before he comes home, it will ease the puppy's transition from the warmth and familiarity of his mom and littermates to the brand-new environment of his new

home and human family. You will be too busy to stock up and prepare your house after your pup comes home, that's for sure! Imagine how a pup must feel upon being transported to a strange new place. It's up to you to comfort him and to let your little pup know that he is going to be happy with you.

FOOD AND WATER BOWLS

Your puppy will need separate bowls for his food and water. Stainless steel pans are generally preferred over plastic bowls since they sterilize better and pups are less inclined to chew on the metal. Heavy-duty ceramic bowls are popular, but consider how often you will have to pick up those heavy bowls. Buy adult-sized bowls, as your puppy will grow into them before you know it.

The breeder introduces solid food to initiate the weaning process. By the time your pup goes home, he will be on a diet of quality puppy food.

THE DOG CRATE

If you think that crates are tools of punishment and confinement for when a dog has misbehaved, think again. Most breeders and almost all trainers recommend a crate as the preferred house-training aid as well as for all-around puppy training and safety. Because dogs are natural den creatures that prefer cave-like environments, the benefits of crate use are many. The crate provides the puppy with his very own "safe house," a cozy place to sleep, take a break or seek comfort with a favorite toy; a travel aid to house your dog when on the road, at motels or at the vet's office; a training aid to help teach your puppy proper toileting habits; a place of solitude when non-dog people happen to drop by and don't want a lively puppy—or even a well-behaved adult dog—

saying hello or begging for their attention.

Crates come in several types, although the wire crate and the fiberglass airline-type crate are the most popular. The wire crates offer better visibility for the pup as well as better ventilation and are the preferred choice for use in the home. Many of the wire crates easily fold down for easy transport. The fiberglass crates, similar to those used by the airlines for animal transport, are sturdier and more den-like, most frequently used as travel crates. However, the fiberglass crates do not collapse and are less ventilated than a wire crate, which can be problematic in hot weather. Some of the newer crates are made of heavy plastic mesh; they are very lightweight and fold up into slim-line suitcases. However, a mesh crate

Blake

might not be suitable for a pup with manic chewing habits.

Don't bother with a puppy-sized crate. Although your Bouvier des Flandres will be a wee fellow when you bring him home, he will grow up in the blink of an eye and your puppy crate will be useless. Purchase a crate that will accommodate an adult Bouvier des Flandres. He will stand up to 27.5 inches tall, depending on sex, so a rather large crate will be necessary. You can use a removable divider panel in the crate to aid in pup's house-training and expand his area as he grows.

BEDDING AND CRATE PADS
Your puppy will enjoy some type of soft bedding in his "room" (the crate), something he can snuggle into to feel cozy and secure. Old towels or blankets are good choices for a young pup, since he may (and probably will) have a toileting accident or two in the crate or decide to chew on the bedding material. Once he is fully trained and out of the early chewing stage, you can replace the puppy bedding with a perma-nent crate pad if you prefer. Crate pads and other dog beds run the gamut from inexpensive to high-end doggie-designer styles, but don't splurge on the good stuff until you are sure that your puppy is reliable and won't tear it up or make a mess on it.

CRATE EXPECTATIONS
To make the crate more inviting to your puppy, you can offer his first meal or two inside the crate, always keeping the crate door open so that he does not feel confined. Keep a favorite toy or two in the crate for him to play with while inside. You can also cover the crate at night with a lightweight sheet to make it more den-like and remove the stimuli of household activity. Never put him into his crate as punishment or as you are scolding him, since he will then associate his crate with negative situations and avoid going there.

PUPPY TOYS
Just as infants and older children require objects to stimulate their minds and bodies, puppies need toys to entertain their curious

TEETHING TIME

All puppies chew. It's normal canine behavior. Chewing just plain feels good to a puppy, especially during the three- to five-month teething period when the adult teeth are breaking through the gums. Rather than attempting to eliminate such a strong natural chewing instinct, you will be more successful if you redirect it and teach your puppy what he may or may not chew. Correct inappropriate chewing with a sharp "No!" and offer him a chew toy, praising him when he takes it. Don't become discouraged. Chewing usually decreases after the adult teeth have come in.

A large and sturdy wire pen is good for supervised outdoor use, as it affords the dog a larger area of safe confinement with full access to fresh air and a view of his surroundings. These pens are collapsible for easy transport.

are cute and look as if they would be a lot of fun, but not all are necessarily safe or good for your puppy, so use caution when you go puppy-toy shopping.

Bouviers are fairly aggressive chewers that enjoy chewing. The best "chewcifiers" are the hardest and strongest nylon and rubber bones, which are safe to gnaw on and come in sizes appropriate for all age groups and breeds. Be especially careful of natural bones, which can splinter or develop dangerous sharp edges; pups can easily swallow or choke on those bone splinters. Veterinarians often tell of surgical nightmares involving bits of splintered bone,

brains, wiggly paws and achy teeth. A fun array of safe doggie toys will help satisfy your puppy's chewing instincts and distract him from gnawing on the leg of your antique chair or your new leather sofa. Most puppy toys

because in addition to the danger of choking, the sharp pieces can damage the intestinal tract.

Similarly, rawhide chews, while a favorite of most dogs and puppies, can be equally dangerous. Pieces of rawhide are easily swallowed after they get soft and gummy from chewing, and dogs have been known to choke on large pieces of ingested rawhide. Rawhide chews should be offered only when you can supervise the puppy.

Soft woolly toys are special puppy favorites. They come in a wide variety of cute shapes and sizes; some look like little stuffed animals. Puppies love to shake

TOYS 'R SAFE

The vast array of tantalizing puppy toys is staggering. Stroll through any pet shop or pet-supply outlet and you will see that the choices can be overwhelming. However, not all dog toys are safe or sensible. Most very young puppies enjoy soft woolly toys that they can snuggle with and carry around. (You know they have outgrown them when they shred them up!) Avoid toys that have buttons, tabs or other enhancements that can be chewed off and swallowed. Soft toys that squeak are fun, but make sure your puppy does not disembowel the toy and remove (and swallow) the squeaker. Toys that rattle or make noise can excite a puppy, but they present the same danger as the squeaky kind and so require supervision. Hard rubber toys that bounce can also entertain a pup, but make sure that the toy is too big for your growing pup to swallow.

Merchandise stands at dog shows offer a wide range of specialty items for dogs as well as novelties for owners who like to collect items featuring the Bouvier.

to your veterinarian might be in order to get his advice and be on the safe side.

An all-time favorite toy for puppies (young and old!) is the empty gallon milk jug. Hard plastic juice containers—46 ounces or more—are also excellent. Such containers make lots of noise when they are batted about, and puppies go crazy with delight as they play with them. However, they don't often last very long, so be sure to remove and replace them when they get chewed up.

A word of caution about homemade toys: be careful with your choices of non-traditional play objects. Never use old shoes or socks, since a puppy cannot distinguish between the old ones on which he's allowed to chew and the new ones in your closet that are strictly off limits. That principle applies to anything that resembles something that you don't want your puppy to chew up.

them up and toss them about, or simply carry them around. Be careful of fuzzy toys that have button eyes or noses that your pup could chew off and swallow, and make sure that he does not disembowel a squeaky toy to remove the squeaker! Braided rope toys are similar in that they are fun to chew and toss around, but they shred easily and the strings are easy to swallow. The strings are not digestible and, if the puppy doesn't pass them in his stool, he could end up at the vet's office. As with rawhides, your puppy should be closely monitored with rope toys.

If you believe that your pup has ingested a piece of one of his toys, check his stools for the next couple of days to see if he passes the item when he defecates. At the same time, also watch for signs of intestinal distress. A call

COLLARS

A lightweight nylon collar is the best choice for a very young pup. Quick-clip collars are easy to put on and remove, and they can be adjusted as the puppy grows. Introduce him to his collar as soon as he comes home to get him accustomed to wearing it. He'll get used to it quickly and won't mind a bit. Make sure that it is snug enough that it won't slip off, yet loose enough to be

COLLARING OUR CANINES

The standard flat collar with a buckle or a snap, in leather, nylon or cotton, is widely regarded as the everyday all-purpose collar. If the collar fits correctly, you should be able to fit two fingers between the collar and the dog's neck.

Leather Buckle Collars

The martingale, Greyhound or limited-slip collar is preferred by many dog owners and trainers. It is fixed with an extra loop that tightens when pressure is applied to the leash. The martingale collar gets tighter but does not "choke" the dog. The limited-slip collar should only be used for walking and training, not for free play or interaction with another dog. These types of collar should never be left on the dog, as the extra loop can lead to accidents.

Choke collars, usually made of stainless steel, are made for training purposes, though are not recommended for small dogs or heavily coated breeds. The chains can injure small dogs or damage long/abundant coats. Thin nylon choke leads are commonly used on show dogs while in the ring, though they are not practical for everyday use.

Limited-Slip Collar

The harness, with two or three straps that attach over the dog's shoulders and around his torso, is a humane and safe alternative to the conventional collar. By and large, a well-made harness is virtually escape-proof. Harnesses are available in nylon and mesh and can be outfitted on most dogs, with chest girths ranging from 10 to 30 inches.

Snap Bolt Choke Collar

Harness

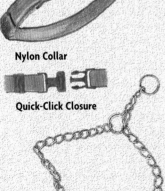

Nylon Collar

Quick-Click Closure

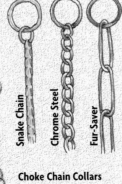

Snake Chain

Chrome Steel

Fur-Saver

Choke Chain Collars

A head collar, composed of a nylon strap that goes around the dog's muzzle and a second strap that wraps around his neck, offers the owner better control over his dog. This device is recommended for problem-solving with dogs (including jumping up, pulling and aggressive behaviors), but must be used with care.

A training halter, including a flat collar and two straps, made of nylon and webbing, is designed for walking. There are several on the market; some are more difficult to put on the dog than others. The halter harness, with two small slip rings at each end, is recommended for ease of use.

comfortable for the pup. You should be able to slip two fingers between the collar and his neck. Check the collar often, as puppies grow in spurts, and his collar can become too tight almost overnight. Training collars should not be used on puppies.

LEASHES

A 6-foot nylon lead is an excellent choice for a young puppy. It is lightweight and not as tempting to chew as a leather lead. You can switch to a 6-foot leather lead after your pup has grown and is used to walking politely on a lead. For initial puppy walks and house-training purposes, you should invest in a shorter lead so that you have more control over the puppy. At first, you don't want him wandering too far away from you, and when taking him out for toileting you will want to keep him in the specific area chosen for his potty spot.

Once the puppy is heel-trained with a traditional leash, you can use a longer leash or consider purchasing a retractable lead. This type of lead is excellent for walking adult dogs that are already leash-wise. The retractable lead allows the dog to roam farther away from you and explore a wider area when out walking, and also retracts when you need to keep him close to you.

HOME SAFETY FOR YOUR PUPPY

The importance of puppy-proofing cannot be overstated. In addition to making your house comfortable for your Bouvier's arrival, you also must make sure that your house is safe for your puppy before you bring him home. There are countless hazards in the owner's personal living environment that a pup can sniff, chew, swallow or destroy. Many are obvious; others are not. Do a thorough advance house check to remove or rearrange those things that could hurt your puppy, keeping any potentially dangerous items out of areas to which he will have access.

KEEP OUT OF REACH

Most dogs don't browse around your medicine cabinet, but accidents do happen! The drug acetaminophen, the active ingredient in Tylenol® and other pain relievers, can be deadly to dogs and cats if ingested in large quantities. Acetaminophen toxicity, caused by the dog's swallowing 15 to 20 tablets, can be manifested in abdominal pains within a day or two of ingestion, as well as liver damage. If you suspect your dog has swiped a bottle of acetaminophen pain reliever, get the dog to the vet immediately so that the vet can induce vomiting and cleanse the dog's stomach.

Electrical cords are especially dangerous, since puppies view them as irresistible chew toys. Unplug and remove all exposed cords or fasten them beneath a baseboard where the puppy cannot reach them. Veterinarians and firefighters can tell you horror stories about electrical burns and house fires that resulted from puppy-chewed electrical cords. Consider this a most serious precaution for your puppy and the rest of your family.

Scout your home for tiny objects that might be seen at a pup's eye level. Keep medication bottles and cleaning supplies well out of reach, and do the same with waste baskets and other trash containers. It goes without saying that you should not use rodent poison or other toxic chemicals in any puppy area and that you must keep such containers safely locked up. You will be amazed at how many places a curious puppy can discover!

Once your house has cleared inspection, check your yard. A sturdy fence, well embedded into the ground, will give your dog a safe place to play and potty.

THE GRASS IS ALWAYS GREENER

Must dog owners decide between their beloved canine pals and their perfectly manicured emerald-green lawns? Just as dog urine is no tonic for growing grass, lawn chemicals are extremely dangerous to your dog. Fertilizers, pesticides and herbicides pose real threats to canines and humans alike. Dogs should be kept off treated grounds for at least 24 hours following treatment. Consider some organic options for your lawn care, such as using a homemade compost or a natural fertilizer instead of a commercial chemical. Some dog-conscious lawnkeepers avoid fertilizers entirely, keeping up their lawns by watering, aerating, mowing and seeding frequently.

As always, dogs complicate the equation. Canines love grass. They roll in it, eat it and love to bury their noses in it—and then do their business in it! Grass can mean hours of feel-good, smell-good fun! In addition to the dangers of lawn-care chemicals, there's also the threat of burs, thorns and pebbles in the grass, not to mention the very common grass allergy. Many dogs develop an incurably itchy skin condition from grass, especially in the late summer when the world is in full bloom.

It's a big world to a small puppy...with a lot to explore! Puppy-proofing and supervision are the keys to your Bouvier pup's safety inside and outside the home.

A Dog-Safe Home

The dog-safety police are taking you and your new puppy on a house tour. Let's go room by room and see how safe your own home is for your new pup. The following items are doggie dangers, so either they must be removed or the dog should be monitored or not have access to these areas.

Living Room
- house plants (some varieties are poisonous)
- fireplace or wood-burning stove
- paint on the walls (lead-based paint is toxic)
- lead drapery weights (toxic lead)
- lamps and electrical cords
- carpet cleaners or deodorizers

Outdoor
- swimming pool
- pesticides
- toxic plants
- lawn fertilizers

Bathroom
- blue water in the toilet bowl
- medicine cabinet (filled with potentially deadly bottles)
- soap bars, bleach, drain cleaners, etc.
- tampons

Kitchen
- household cleaners in the kitchen cabinets
- glass jars and canisters
- sharp objects (like kitchen knives, scissors and forks)
- garbage can (with remnants of good-smelling but dangerous things like onions, potato skins, apple or pear cores, peach pits, coffee beans, etc.)
- "people foods" that are toxic to dogs, like chocolate, raisins, grapes, nuts and onions

Garage
- antifreeze
- fertilizers (including rose foods)
- pesticides and rodenticides
- pool supplies (chlorine and other chemicals)
- oil and gasoline in containers
- sharp objects, electrical cords and power tools

Although Bouviers des Flandres are not known as climbers or fence jumpers, they are still athletic dogs, so a 6-foot-high fence should be adequate to contain an agile youngster or adult. Check the fence periodically for necessary repairs. If there is a weak link or space to squeeze through or under, you can be sure that a determined Bouvier des Flandres will discover it.

The garage and shed can be hazardous places for a pup, as

A healthy pup doesn't just sprout up in the garden! He comes from careful breeding and is maintained by his owner's care and a good vet.

things like fertilizers, chemicals and tools are usually kept there. It's best to keep these areas off-limits to the pup. Antifreeze is especially dangerous to dogs, as they find the taste appealing and it takes only a few licks from the driveway to kill a dog, puppy or adult, small breed or large.

TOXIC PLANTS

Plants are natural puppy magnets, but many can be harmful, even fatal, if ingested by a puppy or adult dog. Scout your yard and home interior and remove any plants, bushes or flowers that could be even mildly dangerous. It could save your puppy's life. You can obtain a complete list of toxic plants from your veterinarian, at the public library or by looking online.

VISITING THE VETERINARIAN

A good veterinarian is your Bouvier des Flandres puppy's best health-insurance policy. If you do not already have a vet, ask friends and experienced dog people in your area for recommendations so that you can select a vet before you bring your Bouvier des Flandres puppy home. Make sure that your chosen vet is knowledgeable about and experienced with large breeds. Also arrange for

PUPPY PARASITES

Parasites are nasty little critters that live in or on your dog or puppy. Most puppies are born with ascarid roundworms, which are acquired from dormant ascarids residing in the dam. Other parasites can be acquired through contact with infected fecal matter. Take a stool sample to your vet for testing. He will prescribe a safe wormer to treat any parasites found in your puppy's stool. Always have a fecal test performed at your puppy's annual veterinary exam.

your puppy's first veterinary examination beforehand, since many vets have two- and three-week waiting periods and your puppy should visit the vet within a day or so of coming home.

It's important to make sure your puppy's first visit to the vet is a pleasant and positive one. The vet should take great care to befriend the pup and handle him gently to make their first meeting a positive experience. The vet will give the pup a thorough physical examination and set up a schedule for vaccinations and other neces-sary wellness visits. Be sure to show your vet any health and inoc-ulation records, which you should have received from your breeder. Your vet is a great source of canine health information, so be sure to ask questions and take notes. Creating a health journal for your

puppy will make a handy reference for his wellness and any future health problems that may arise.

MEETING THE FAMILY

Your Bouvier's homecoming is an exciting time for all members of the family, and it's only natural that everyone will be eager to meet him, pet him and play with him. However, for the puppy's sake, it's best to make these initial family meetings as uneventful as possible so that the pup is not overwhelmed with too much too soon. Remember, he has just left his dam and his littermates and is away from the breeder's home for the first time. Despite his fuzzy wagging tail, he is still apprehensive and wondering where he is and who all these strange humans are. He needs affection, attention and supervision, but it's best to let him explore on his own and meet the family members as he feels comfortable. Let him investigate all the new smells, sights and sounds at his own pace. Children should be especially careful to not get overly excited, use loud voices or hug the pup too tightly. Be calm, gentle and affectionate, and be ready to comfort him if he appears frightened or uneasy.

Be sure to show your puppy his new crate during this first day home. Toss a treat or two inside the crate; if he associates the crate with food, he will associate the crate with good things. If he is comfortable with the crate, you can offer him his first meal inside it. Leave the door ajar so he can wander in and out as he chooses.

FIRST NIGHT IN HIS NEW HOME

So much has happened in your Bouvier des Flandres puppy's first day away from the breeder. He's had his first car ride to his new home. He's met his new human family and perhaps the other family pets. He has explored his new house and yard, at least those places where he is to be allowed during his first weeks at home. He may have visited his new veterinarian. He has eaten his first meal or two away from his dam and littermates. Surely that's enough to tire out an eight-week-old Bouvier des Flandres pup...or so you hope!

It's bedtime. During the day, the pup investigated his crate, which is his new den and sleeping space, so it is not entirely strange to him. Line the crate with a soft towel or blanket that he can snuggle into and gently place him into the crate for the night. Some breeders send home a piece of bedding from where the pup slept with his littermates, and those familiar scents are a great comfort for the puppy on his first night without his siblings.

He will probably whine or cry. The puppy is objecting to the

confinement and the fact that he is alone for the first time. This can be a stressful time for you as well as for the pup. It's important that you remain strong and don't let the puppy out of his crate to comfort him. He will fall asleep eventually. If you release him, the puppy will learn that crying means "out" and will continue that habit. You are laying the groundwork for future habits. Some breeders find that soft music can soothe a crying pup and help him get to sleep.

On his first night in his new home, your pup may miss the companionship of his littermates and feel a bit lonely.

SOCIALIZING YOUR PUPPY

The first 20 weeks, especially between 8 and 12 weeks old, of your Bouvier des Flandres puppy's life are the most important of his entire lifetime. A properly socialized puppy will grow up to be a confident and stable adult who will be a pleasure to live with and a welcome addition to the neighborhood. The importance of social-

THE FAMILY FELINE

A resident cat has feline squatter's rights. The cat will treat the newcomer (your puppy) as she sees fit, regardless of what you do or say. So it's best to let the two of them work things out on their own terms. Cats have a height advantage and will generally leap to higher ground to avoid direct contact with a rambunctious pup. Some will hiss and boldly swat at a pup who passes by or tries to reach the cat. Keep the puppy under control in the presence of the cat and they will eventually become accustomed to each other.

Here's a hint: move the cat's litter box where the puppy can't get into it! It's best to do so well before the pup comes home so the cat is used to the new location.

ization cannot be overemphasized. Research on canine behavior has proven that puppies who are not exposed to new sights, sounds, people and animals during their first 20 weeks of life will grow up to be timid and fearful, even aggressive, and unable to flourish outside of their home environment.

Socializing your puppy is not difficult and, in fact, will be a fun time for you both. Lead training goes hand in hand with socialization, so your puppy will be learning how to walk on a lead at the same time that he's meeting the neighborhood. Because the Bouvier des Flandres is such a terrific breed, everyone will enjoy meeting "the new kid on the block." Take him for short walks, to the park and to other dog-friendly places where he will encounter new people, especially children. Puppies automatically recognize children as "little people" and are drawn to play with them. Just make sure that you supervise these meetings and that the children do not get too rough or encourage him to play too hard. An overzealous pup can often nip too hard, frightening the child and in turn making the puppy overly excited. A bad experience in puppyhood can impact a dog for life, so a pup that has a negative experience with a child may grow up to be shy or even aggressive around children.

Take your puppy along on your daily errands. Puppies are natural "people magnets," and most people who see your pup will want to pet him. All of these encounters will help to mold him into a confident adult dog.

Likewise, you will soon feel like a confident, responsible dog owner, rightly proud of your mannerly Bouvier des Flandres.

Be especially careful of your puppy's encounters and experiences during the eight-to-ten-week-old period, which is also called the "fear period." This is a serious imprinting period, and all contact during this time should be gentle and positive. A frightening or negative event could leave a permanent impression that could affect his future behavior if a similar situation arises.

Also make sure that your puppy has received his first and second rounds of vaccinations before you expose him to other dogs or bring him to places that other dogs may frequent. Avoid dog parks and other strange-dog areas until your vet assures you that your puppy is fully immunized and resistant to the diseases that can be passed between canines. Discuss socialization with your breeder, as some breeders recommend socializing the puppy even before he has received all of his inoculations, depending on how outgoing the puppy may be.

LEADER OF THE PUPPY'S PACK
Like other canines, your puppy needs an authority figure, someone he can look up to and regard as the leader of his "pack." His first pack leader was his dam,

The one who feeds is the one who leads—with a pack of pups, at least!

who taught him to be polite and not chew too hard on her ears or nip at her muzzle. He learned those same lessons from his littermates. If he played too rough, they cried in pain and stopped the game, which sent an important message to the rowdy puppy.

As puppies play together, they are also struggling to determine who will be the boss. Being pack animals, dogs need someone to be in charge. If a litter of puppies remained together beyond puppyhood, one of the pups would emerge as the strongest one, the one who calls the shots.

Once your puppy leaves the pack, he will look intuitively for a new leader. If he does not recog-

Early socialization begins among littermates, which is why the time prior to leaving the breeder is so crucial to each pup's personality development.

nize you as that leader, he will try to assume that position for himself. Of course, it is hard to imagine your adorable Bouvier des Flandres puppy trying to be in charge when he is so small and seemingly helpless. You must remember that these are natural canine instincts. Do not cave in and allow your pup to get the upper "paw"!

Just as socialization is so important during these first 20 weeks, so too is your puppy's early education. He was born without any bad habits. He does not know what is good or bad behavior. If he does things like nipping and digging, it's because he is having fun and doesn't know that humans consider these things as "bad." It's your job to teach him proper puppy manners, and this is the best time to accomplish that…before he has developed bad habits, since it is much more difficult to "unlearn" or correct unacceptable learned behavior than to teach good behavior from the start.

Make sure that all members of the family understand the importance of being consistent when training their new puppy. If you tell the puppy to stay off the sofa and your daughter allows him to cuddle on the couch with her to watch her favorite TV show, your pup will be confused about what he is and is not allowed to do. Have a family conference before your pup comes home so that everyone understands the basic principles of puppy training and the rules you have set forth for the pup, and agrees to follow them.

The old adage that "an ounce of prevention is worth a pound of cure" is especially true when it comes to puppies. It is much easier to prevent inappropriate behavior than it is to change it. It's also easier and less stressful for the pup, since it will keep discipline to a minimum and create a more positive learning environment for him. That, in turn, will also be easier on you.

SOLVING PUPPY PROBLEMS

CHEWING AND NIPPING
Nipping at fingers and toes is normal puppy behavior. Chewing is also the way that puppies investigate their surroundings. However, you will have to teach your puppy that chewing anything other than his toys is not acceptable. That won't happen overnight and at times puppy

teeth will test your patience. However, if you allow nipping and chewing to continue, just think about the damage that a mature Bouvier des Flandres can do with a full set of adult teeth.

Whenever your puppy nips your hand or fingers, cry out "Ouch!" in a loud voice, which should startle your puppy and stop him from nipping, even if only for a moment. Immediately distract him by offering a small treat or an appropriate toy for him to chew instead (which means having chew toys and puppy treats handy or in your pockets at all times). Praise him when he takes the toy and tell him what a good fellow he is. Praise is just as or even more important in puppy training as discipline and correction.

Puppies also tend to nip at children more often than adults, since they perceive little ones to

Too hard to be a chew toy, too slow to chase...this perplexed pup wonders what to do with his hard-shelled playmate!

be more vulnerable and more similar to their littermates. Teach your children appropriate responses to nipping behavior. If they are unable to handle it themselves, you may have to intervene. Puppy nips can be quite painful and a child's frightened reaction will only encourage a puppy to nip harder, which is a natural canine response. As with all other puppy situations, interaction between your Bouvier des Flandres puppy and children should be supervised.

Chewing on objects, not just family members' fingers and ankles, is also normal canine behavior that can be especially tedious (for the owner, not the pup) during the teething period when the puppy's adult teeth are coming in. At this stage, chewing just plain feels good. Furniture legs and cabinet corners are common puppy favorites. Shoes and other personal items also taste pretty good to a pup.

CREATE A SCHEDULE

Puppies thrive on sameness and routine. Offer meals at the same time each day, take him out at regular times for potty trips and do the same for play periods and outdoor activity. Make note of when your puppy naps and when he is most lively and energetic, and try to plan his day around those times. Once he is house-trained and more predictable in his habits, he will be better able to tolerate changes in his schedule.

Being a puppy is exhausting! These Bouvier siblings curl up to take a break...until it's playtime again!

period, and the furniture could sustain a nasty nick or two. These can be trying times, so be prepared for those inevitable accidents and comfort yourself in knowing that this too shall pass.

JUMPING UP

Puppies will be puppies, and puppies jump up...on you, your guests, your counters and your furniture. Just another normal part of growing up, and one you need to meet head-on before it becomes an ingrained habit. Imagine how a visitor to your home would react if greeted in this manner by 70 pounds of Bouvier!

The key to jump correction is consistency. You cannot correct your Bouvier des Flandres for jumping up on you today, then allow it to happen tomorrow by greeting him with hugs and kisses. As you have learned by now, consistency is critical to all puppy lessons.

For starters, try turning your back as soon as the puppy jumps. Jumping up is a means of gaining your attention and, if the pup can't see your face, he may get discouraged and learn that he loses eye contact with his beloved master when he jumps up.

Leash corrections also work, and most puppies respond well to a leash tug if they jump. Grasp the leash close to the puppy's collar and give a quick tug downward, using the command "Off."

The best solution is, once again, prevention. If you value something, keep it tucked away and out of reach. You can't hide your dining-room table in a closet, but you can try to deflect the chewing by applying a bitter product made just to deter dogs from chewing. Available in a spray or cream, this substance is vile-tasting, although safe for dogs, and most puppies will avoid the forbidden object after one tiny taste. You also can apply the product to your leash if the puppy tries to chew on his leash during training sessions.

Keep a ready supply of safe chews handy to offer your Bouvier des Flandres as a distraction when he starts to chew on something that's a "no-no." Remember, at this tender age he does not yet know what is permitted or forbidden, so you have to be "on call" every minute he's awake and on the prowl.

You may lose a treasure or two during puppy's growing-up

Do not use the word "Down," since "Down" is used to teach the puppy to lie down, which is a separate action that he will learn during his education in the basic commands. As soon as the puppy has backed off, tell him to sit and immediately praise him for doing so. This will take many repetitions and won't be accomplished quickly, so don't get discouraged or give up; you must be even more persistent than your puppy.

A second method used for jump correction is the spritzer bottle. Fill a spray bottle with water mixed with a bit of lemon juice or vinegar. As soon as puppy jumps, command him "Off" and spritz him with the water mixture. Of course, that means having the spray bottle handy whenever or wherever jumping usually happens.

Yet a third method to discourage jumping is grasping the puppy's paws and holding them gently but firmly until he struggles to get away. Wait a brief moment or two, then release his paws and give him a command to sit. He should eventually learn that jumping gets him into an uncomfortable predicament.

Children are major victims of puppy jumping, since puppies view little people as ready targets for jumping up as well as nipping. If your children (or their friends) are unable to dispense jump corrections, you will have to intervene and handle it for them.

Important to prevention is also knowing what you should not do. Never kick your Bouvier (for any reason, not just for jumping) or knock him in the chest with your knee. That maneuver could actually harm your puppy. Vets can tell you stories about puppies who suffered broken bones after being banged about when they jumped up.

"Counter Surfing"

What we like to call "counter surfing" is a normal extension of jumping and usually starts to happen as soon as a puppy realizes that he is big enough to stand on his hind legs and investigate the good stuff on the kitchen counter or the coffee table. Once again, you have to be there to prevent it! As soon as you see your Bouvier des Flandres even start to raise himself up, startle him with a sharp "No!" or "Aaahh, aaahh!" If he succeeds and manages to get one or both paws on the forbidden surface, tell him "Off!" and place his front feet back on the floor if necessary. As soon as he's back on all four paws, command him to sit and praise at once.

For surf prevention, make sure to keep any tempting treats or edibles out of reach, where your Bouvier des Flandres can't see or smell them. It's the old rule of prevention yet again.

Adding a Bouvier des Flandres to your household means adding a new family member who will need your care each and every day. When your Bouvier des Flandres pup first comes home, you will start a routine with him so that, as he grows up, your dog will have a daily schedule just as you do. The aspects of your dog's daily care will likewise become regular parts of your day, so you'll both have a new schedule. Dogs learn by consistency and thrive on routine: regular times for meals, exercise, grooming and potty trips are just as important for your dog as they are to you! Your dog's schedule will depend much on your family's daily routine, but remember that you now have a new member of the family who is part of your day every day.

FEEDING

Feeding your Bouvier the best diet is based on various factors, including age, activity level, overall condition and size of breed. When you visit the breeder, he will share with you his advice about the proper diet for your dog based on his experience with the breed and the foods with which he has had success. Likewise, your vet will be a helpful source of advice throughout the dog's life and will aid you in planning a diet for optimal health.

FEEDING THE PUPPY

Of course, your pup's very first food will be his dam's milk. There

What to feed? With such an array of choices, rely on the advice of your breeder and vet.

may be special situations in which pups fail to nurse, necessitating that the breeder hand-feed them with a formula, but for the most part pups spend the first weeks of life nursing from their dam. The breeder weans the pups by gradually introducing solid foods and decreasing the milk meals. Pups may even start themselves off on the weaning process, albeit inadvertently, if they snatch bites from their mom's food bowl.

By the time the pups are ready for new homes, they are fully weaned and eating a good puppy food. As a new owner, you may be thinking, "Great! The breeder has taken care of the hard part." Not so fast.

A puppy's first year of life is the time when all or most of his growth and development takes place. This is a delicate time, and diet plays a huge role in proper skeletal and muscular formation. Improper diet and exercise habits can lead to damaging problems that will compromise the dog's health and movement for his entire life. That being said, new owners should not worry needlessly. With the myriad types of food formulated specifically for growing pups of different-sized breeds, dog-food manufacturers have taken much of the guesswork out of feeding your puppy well. Since growth-food formulas are designed to provide the nutrition that a growing puppy needs, it is

unnecessary and, in fact, can prove harmful to add supplements to the diet. Research has shown that too much of certain vitamin supplements and minerals predispose a dog to skeletal problems. It's by no means a case of "if a little is good, a lot is better." At every stage of your dog's life, too much or too little in the way of nutrients can be harmful, which is why a manufactured complete food is the easiest way to know that your dog is getting what he needs. For a large-breed pup like the Bouvier, a proper diet promotes healthy, not rapid, growth.

Because of a young pup's small body and accordingly small digestive system, his daily portion will be divided up into small meals throughout the day. This can mean starting off with three or more meals a day and decreasing the number of meals as the pup matures. It is generally thought,

There is nothing better for a newborn puppy than his mother's milk.

NOT HUNGRY?

No dog in his right mind would turn down his dinner, would he? If you notice that your dog has lost interest in his food, there could be any number of causes. Dental problems are a common cause of appetite loss, one that is often overlooked. If your dog has a toothache, a loose tooth or sore gums from infection, chances are it doesn't feel so good to chew. Think about when you've had a toothache! If your dog does not approach the food bowl with his usual enthusiasm, look inside his mouth for signs of a problem. Whatever the cause, you'll want to consult your vet so that your chow hound can get back to his happy, hungry self as soon as possible.

condition, but extra weight can strain a pup's developing frame, causing skeletal problems.

Watch your Bouvier's weight as he grows and, if the recommended amounts seem to be too much or too little for your pup, consult the vet about appropriate dietary changes. Keep in mind that treats, although small, can quickly add up throughout the day, contributing unnecessary calories. Treats are fine when used prudently; opt for dog treats specially formulated to be healthy or for nutritious snacks like small pieces of cheese or cooked chicken.

FEEDING THE ADULT DOG

For the adult (meaning physically mature) dog, feeding properly is about maintenance, not growth. Again, correct weight is a concern. Your dog should appear fit and should have an evident "waist." His ribs should not be protruding (a sign of being underweight), but they should be covered by only a slight layer of fat. Under normal circumstances, an adult dog can be maintained fairly easily with a high-quality nutritionally complete adult-formula food. A Bouvier is large, but should be an agile, not too heavy, dog.

Factor treats into your dog's overall daily caloric intake, and avoid offering table scraps. Not only are certain "people foods," like chocolate, onions, grapes,

especially with bloat-prone breeds, that dividing the grown dog's daily portion into two meals on a morning/evening schedule, rather than one large meal, is healthier for the dog's digestion.

Regarding the feeding schedule, feeding the pup at the same times and in the same place each day is important for both housebreaking purposes and establishing the dog's everyday routine. As for the amount to feed, growing puppies generally need proportionately more food per body weight than their adult counterparts, but a pup should never be allowed to gain excess weight. Dogs of all ages should be kept in proper body

raisins and nuts, toxic to dogs, but feeding from the table encourages begging and overeating. Overweight dogs are more prone to health problems. Research has even shown that obesity takes years off a dog's life. With that in mind, resist the urge to overfeed and over-treat. Don't make unnecessary additions to your dog's diet, whether with tidbits or with extra vitamins and minerals.

The amount of food needed for proper maintenance will vary depending on the individual dog's activity level, but you will be able to tell whether the daily portions are keeping him in good shape. With the wide variety of good complete foods available, choosing what to feed is largely a matter of personal preference. Just as with the puppy, the adult dog should have consistency in his mealtimes and feeding place. In addition to a consistent routine, regular mealtimes also allow the owner to see how much his dog is eating and notice changes in his appetite that could mean a health problem, as well as to implement bloat preventives, which would be impossible if the dog has been allowed to eat at will.

DIETS FOR THE AGING DOG

A good rule of thumb is that once a dog has reached 75% of his expected lifespan, he has reached "senior citizen" or geriatric status. Your Bouvier des Flandres will be

DIET DON'TS

- Got milk? Don't give it to your dog! Dogs cannot tolerate large quantities of cows' milk, as they do not have the enzymes to digest lactose.
- You may have heard of dog owners who add raw eggs to their dogs' food for a shiny coat or to make the food more palatable, but consumption of raw eggs too often can cause a deficiency of the vitamin biotin.
- Avoid feeding table scraps, as they will upset the balance of the dog's complete food. Additionally, fatty or highly seasoned foods can cause upset canine stomachs.
- Do not offer raw meat to your dog. Raw meat can contain parasites; it also is high in fat.
- Vitamin A toxicity in dogs can be caused by too much raw liver, especially if the dog already gets enough vitamin A in his balanced diet, which should be the case.
- Bones like chicken, pork chop and other soft bones are not suitable, as they easily splinter.

What Is "Bloat"?

Need yet another reason to avoid tossing your dog a morsel from your plate? It is shown that dogs fed table scraps have an increased risk of developing bloat, or gastric torsion. Did you know that more occurrences of bloat occur in the warm-weather months due to the frequency of outdoor cooking and dining and dogs' receiving "samples" from the fired-up grill?

You likely have heard the term "bloat," which refers to gastric torsion (gastric dilatation/volvulus), a potentially fatal condition. As it is directly related to feeding and exercise practices, a brief explanation here is warranted. The term *dilatation* means that the dog's stomach is filled with air, while *volvulus* means that the stomach is twisted around on itself, blocking the entrance/exit points. Dilatation/volvulus is truly a deadly combination, although they also can occur independently of each other. An affected dog cannot digest food or pass gas, and blood cannot flow to the stomach, causing accumulation of toxins and gas, great pain and shock, progressing to death if untreated.

Many theories exist on what exactly causes bloat, but we do know that deep-chested breeds are more prone. Activities like eating a large meal, gulping water, strenuous exercise too close to mealtimes or a combination of these factors can contribute to bloat, though not every case is directly related to these more well-known causes. With that in mind, we can focus on incorporating simple daily preventives and knowing how to recognize the symptoms. Affected dogs need immediate veterinary attention, as death can result quickly. Signs include obvious restlessness/discomfort, crying in pain, drooling/excessive salivation, unproductive attempts to vomit or relieve himself, visibly bloated appearance and collapsing. Do not wait: get to the vet *right away* if you see any of these symptoms. The vet will confirm by x-ray if the stomach is bloated with air; if so, the dog must be treated *immediately*.

A bloated dog will be treated for shock, and the stomach must be relieved of the air pressure as well as surgically returned to its correct position. If part of the stomach wall has died, that part must be removed. Usually the stomach is stapled to the abdominal wall to prevent another episode of bloating; this may or may not be successful. The vet should also check the dog for heart problems related to the condition.

considered a senior at about 7 years of age; he has a projected lifespan of about 10–12 years. (The smallest breeds generally enjoy the longest lives and the largest breeds the shortest.)

Your Bouvier will require some dietary changes to accommodate the changes that come along with increased age. One change is that the older dog's dietary needs become more similar to that of a puppy. Specifically, dogs can metabolize more protein as youngsters and seniors than in the adult-maintenance stage. Discuss with your vet whether you need to switch to a higher-protein or senior-formulated food or whether your current adult-dog food contains sufficient nutrition for the senior.

Watching the dog's weight remains essential, even more so in

BLOAT-PREVENTION TIPS

As varied as the causes of bloat are the tips for prevention, but some common preventive methods follow:

▶ Feed two or three small meals daily rather than one large one;

▶ Do not feed water before, after or with meals, but allow access to water at all other times;

▶ Never permit rapid eating or gulping of water;

▶ No exercise for the dog at least two hours before and (especially) after meals;

▶ Feed high-quality food with adequate protein, adequate fiber content and not too much fat and carbohydrate;

▶ Explore herbal additives, enzymes or gas-reduction products (only under a vet's advice) to encourage a "friendly" environment in the dog's digestive system;

▶ Avoid foods and ingredients known to produce gas;

▶ Avoid stressful situations for the dog, especially at mealtimes;

▶ Make dietary changes gradually, over a period of a few weeks;

▶ Do not feed dry food only;

▶ Although the role of genetics as a causative of bloat is not known, many breeders do not breed from previously affected dogs;

▶ Sometimes owners are advised to have gastroplexy (stomach stapling) performed on their dogs as a preventive measure.

Of utmost importance is that you know your dog! Pay attention to his behavior and any changes that could be symptomatic of bloat. Your dog's life depends on it!

the senior stage. Older dogs are already more vulnerable to illness, and obesity only contributes to their susceptibility to problems. As the older dog becomes less active and, thus, exercises less, his regular portions may cause him to gain weight. At this point, you may consider decreasing his daily food intake or switching to a reduced-calorie food. As with other changes, you should consult your vet for advice.

DON'T FORGET THE WATER!

Regardless of what type of food your Bouvier eats, there's no doubt that he needs plenty of water. Fresh cold water, in a clean bowl, should be made available to your dog. There are special circumstances, such as during puppy housebreaking, when you will want to monitor your pup's water intake so that you will be able to predict when he will need to relieve himself, but water must

be available to him nonetheless. Water is essential for hydration and proper body function just as it is in humans.

You will get to know how much your dog typically drinks in a day. Of course, in the heat or if exercising vigorously, he will be more thirsty and will drink more. However, if he begins to drink noticeably more water for no apparent reason, this could signal any of various problems, and you are advised to consult your vet.

A word of caution concerning your deep-chested dog's water intake: he should never be allowed to gulp water, especially at mealtimes. In fact, his water intake should be limited at meal-times as a rule. This simple daily precaution can go a long way in protecting your dog from the dangerous and potentially fatal gastric torsion (bloat).

EXERCISE

We all know the importance of exercise for humans, so it should come as no surprise that it is essential for our canine friends as well. Now, regardless of your own level of fitness, get ready to assume the role of personal trainer for your Bouvier. It's not as hard as it sounds, and it will have health benefits for you, too.

Just as with anything else you do with your dog, you must set a routine for his exercise. It's the same as your daily morning run

Water is as important to your dog's diet as good-quality food.

before work or never missing the 7 p.m. aerobics class. If you plan it and get into the habit of actually doing it, it will become just another part of your day. Think of it as making daily exercise appointments with your dog, and stick to your schedule.

As a rule, dogs in normal health should have at least a half-hour of activity each day, allowing at least two hours between exercise and mealtimes (before and after). Dogs with health or orthopedic problems may have specific limitations, so their exercise plans are best devised with the help of a vet. For healthy dogs, there are many ways to fit 30 minutes of activity into your day. Depending on your schedule, you may plan a 15-minute walk or activity session in the morning and again in the

A Bouvier in fit condition appears muscular and athletic, not bulky and lumbering.

evening, or do it all at once in a half-hour session each day. Walking is the most popular way to exercise a dog (it's good for you, too!); other suggestions include retrieving games, jogging and disc-catching or other active games with his toys. If you have a safe body of water nearby and a dog that likes to swim, swimming is an excellent form of exercise for dogs, putting no stress on his frame. Introductions to water must be done carefully.

For overweight dogs, dietary changes and activity will help the goal of weight loss. While they should of course be encouraged to be active, remember not to overdo it, as the excess weight is already putting strain on his vital organs and bones. Bouviers of all ages will enjoy time spent with their owners, doing things together.

PUPPY STEPS

Puppies are brimming with activity and enthusiasm. It seems that they can play all day and night without tiring, but don't overdo your puppy's exercise regimen. Easy does it for the puppy's first six to nine months. Keep walks brief and don't let the puppy engage in stressful jumping games. The puppy frame is delicate, and too much exercise during those critical growing months can cause injury to his bone structure, ligaments and musculature. Save his first jog for his first birthday!

While the Bouvier is a working dog that should have a natural appearance, much grooming is required to keep the coat in top condition and to accent the breed's very distinctive silhouette.

Regardless of your dog's condition and activity level, exercise offers benefits to all dogs and owners. Consider the fact that dogs who are kept active are more stimulated both physically and mentally, meaning that they are less likely to become bored and lapse into destructive behavior. Also consider the benefits of one-on-one time with your dog every day, continually strengthening the bond between the two of you. Furthermore, exercising together will improve health and longevity for both of you. You both need exercise, and now you and your dog have a workout partner and motivator!

GROOMING

BASIC COAT MAINTENANCE

Grooming the Bouvier's coat should be a pleasant task, not only to make your dog more beautiful but also to keep his skin and coat healthy. The coat of the Bouvier requires a great deal of maintenance. Even a pet Bouvier, who will never enter the show ring, must be thoroughly groomed, and this requires time and skill.

Begin grooming when your Bouvier is a puppy, using a grooming table, preferably with an arm to which you can attach his leash so that he will be secure on the table. Remember that you cannot leave your dog unattended on the grooming table, not even for a quick task like answering the phone! If he tries to jump from the table while fastened to the grooming arm, he will be left dangling in mid-air (or topple the table over) and will surely injure himself. Likewise, if he is not fastened, he can injure himself if he jumps or falls from the table.

Daily grooming is well advised. It stimulates the blood circulation, avoids mats and tangles and guarantees good coat condition. It is also beneficial for the dog's character, as he bonds with his groomer (you!) and learns to submit to your authority. In this sense, grooming is a part of basic socialization and obedience training. Bouviers normally enjoy brushing and combing, but some dominant dogs may resist; therefore, you should introduce the grooming routine as soon as you acquire your new puppy.

Basic grooming of an adult dog requires that you brush and comb your dog once or twice weekly at the minimum. This routine groom-

WATER SHORTAGE

No matter how well behaved your dog is, bathing is always a project! Nothing can substitute for a good warm bath, but owners do have the option of giving their dogs "dry" baths. Pet shops sell excellent products, in both powder and spray forms, designed for spot-cleaning your dog. These dry shampoos are convenient for touch-up jobs when you don't have the time to bathe your dog in the traditional way.

Muddy feet, messy behinds and smelly coats can be spot-cleaned and deodorized with a "wet-nap"-style cleaner. On those days when your dog insists on rolling in fresh goose droppings and there's no time for a bath, a spot bath can save the day. These pre-moistened wipes are also handy for other grooming needs like wiping faces, ears and eyes and freshening tails and behinds.

ing should be established as a simple ritual, always using the same technique and order in which you do things.

If you have a dog with a rather harsh coat, you can start with hand-stripping or plucking, which means that you remove dead hair by pulling it out with your forefinger and thumb. Alternatively, you can use a stripping knife with an adjustable blade. Several variations of this knife are on the market. The teeth of the knife, which are small, must not be too sharp. You should use a coarse knife, especially if the coat is rather soft. Remove the hair by plucking with a stripping knife and your thumb, pulling from the roots, not by cutting. Don't remove too many hairs at a time, as this can be painful, and always pull in the direction in which the hair grows. Finer stripping knives can also be used as cutting tools for modeling the coat. If you've never attempted stripping, have a breeder or groomer help you get started.

After stripping, you can then brush your Bouvier with a stiff bristle or pin brush, the latter having rigid metal pins that are spaced rather far apart and set in a rubber pad. You can start at the head, continue with the body and finally brush the legs. Always brush the body parts in the same order each time that you groom. Make certain that you are not just brushing the surface of the coat, but that the coat separates all the way to the skin. After a thorough brushing, you can comb through the coat, using a comb with medium- or wide-spaced teeth. When the teeth of the comb are too close together, the comb will neither pass through the coat easily nor get all the way down to the skin.

Regarding shedding problems, contrary to what you may expect with a hairy dog such as the Bouvier, you will find very little

A Bouvier puppy getting his first trim.

Electric clippers are used on the head, while straight scissors are used to trim around the edges of the ears.

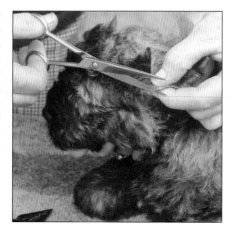

Puppies must become accustomed to grooming while young so that they learn to tolerate the process and stand still, especially during scissor work.

loose hair in the house when you groom the dog regularly.

If you think you are not up to the job of grooming or trimming your dog, it is best for you to seek help. You can ask your breeder if he can help you by showing you the grooming or trimming procedure. There are several types of grooming—pet, utility and show grooming, also called "competition grooming." Show or competition grooming is an art and requires a great deal of skill. Beauty salons for dogs are often not the best places to take your Bouvier to be groomed for competition. For the most part, only your breeder or a professional handler will know enough about Bouvier show grooming to produce satisfactory results. If you bought a Bouvier who eventually will be a show dog, he should be groomed for competition, at least initially, by your breeder or someone experienced enough in the breed to know what is expected of a show Bouvier's coat. Eventually you can learn to groom your Bouvier for the show ring yourself, if you are interested in doing so.

TRIMMING FOR THE SHOW RING
It is difficult to give a good definition of trimming. In essence it means making the coat presentable, orderly and neat, with the aid of cutting or clipping. Trimming dogs can be quite involved, and usually includes preliminary

procedures such as bathing, brushing, combing, stripping, plucking and coat conditioning. The actual trimming process involves the shaping or modeling of the coat. Perhaps the best definition of trimming, with regard to dogs, is to "barber the coat in order to create a desired appearance." This desired appearance is the breed's general appearance as described in the official breed standard. Therefore, if you intend to show your Bouvier, you must understand what the breed standard calls for.

The Bouvier's type depends on his general outline or silhouette. By proper show grooming, the coat can be "shaped," which means that the silhouette can be made to appear more typical. However, in some major Bouvier standards, including the FCI's and the British, grooming is not recommended or even mentioned; rather, the coat is described as being neither too long nor too short, about 6 cm (2.5 in) in length. The American standard mentions "top coat trimmed if necessary," but it also includes these very important comments: "The coat may be trimmed slightly only to accent the body line" and "Overtrimming which alters the natural rugged appearance is to be avoided." Nevertheless, and perhaps unfortunately, with the realities of showing, a bit more grooming is needed than the standards may suggest, so as to give the Bouvier an attractive appear-

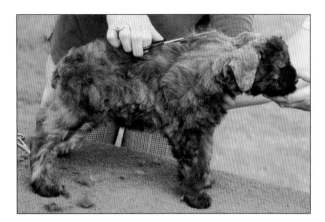

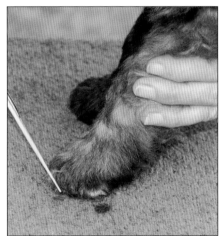

ABOVE: The coat on the back is trimmed, following the pup's natural outline. LEFT: Excess hair on the foot is trimmed to accentuate the round shape.

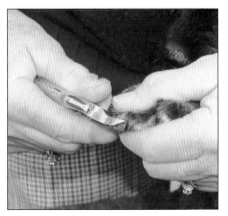

Nail clipping adds to the foot's neat appearance.

A complete grooming routine is more than just coat care. Ears are gently cleaned with a cotton wipe.

The areas around the eyes are cleaned, also by wiping with soft cotton.

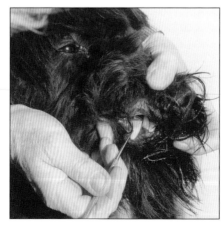

Dental hygiene is best accomplished through regular toothbrushing and occasional use of a dental scraper, which your vet can show you how to use properly.

ance and make him more competitive in the show ring.

You can certainly learn to groom your Bouvier, puppy or adult, for the show ring. However, bear in mind that it can take a long time to learn the show trim, and even longer to get it right, and that even a talented person can become discouraged.

Your breeder may introduce you to basic grooming and can be a wonderful resource for learning how to groom for the show ring. As your skills improve, you will likely find it fun and a good way to save money. When you go to shows, you can study the trims of top-winning dogs. Talk with breeders, experienced exhibitors and professional handlers and groomers, and ask for advice when they have a free moment. Ask specific questions so that you sound like you have begun your Bouvier education and have taken on some responsibility for properly grooming and caring for your dog's coat.

Most owners and breeders have their own version of how to trim and care for their Bouviers' coats. You will find out that there are several methods and many different opinions on the subject. The following briefly outlined step-by-step procedure can serve as a guide to the overall trimming process. A good knowledge of the breed standard is necessary; you should always keep in mind the ideal silhouette or outline of a show Bouvier and should try to model your dog accordingly.

Start with the head, which is the most difficult part of the trimming process. Clip the skull first, from the occiput to the eyebrows. The eyebrows should not be removed; they should be shortened a little and combed forward, down over the muzzle, but without veiling the eyes completely. The beard and mustache should be brushed and combed, trimming only the overly long hairs. The hair on the sides of the skull should be shortened a little and the cheek hairs thinned out, so as to join well with the outside corner of the ear and the hair on the muzzle. The ears are shaved, inside and outside, but the outside should be in line with the neck.

The hair around the neck is very thick and should be combed before trimming. Then cut and trim evenly, starting at the jaw line and working downward, with a smooth transition to the forechest, the withers and the shoulders. The hair on the chest and the body should be rather short, but may be a little longer on the forechest. The hair on the topline, from the back to the tail, should be short and level, blending to a fuller coat on the sides of the chest and the flanks. The (docked) tail is clipped quite close. The underline, from the brisket (lower chest) to the abdomen or belly, should have only a slight only

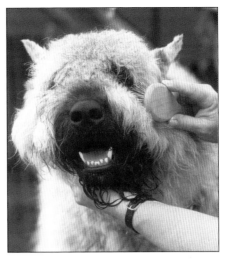

While the faces of many breeds do not carry much coat, the Bouvier's facial furnishings are long and a trademark of the breed, requiring special attention to grooming.

rise, which means that the abdomen should be only slightly tucked-up and trimming should follow this natural line.

The hind legs are trimmed short from under the tail, leaving the hair longer down on the legs,

You may choose to purchase a hair dryer made for dogs. Regardless of what type of dryer you use, it should be on a low heat setting, as dogs' skin is quite sensitive.

LEFT: Grooming should be performed with the pup on a sturdy grooming table with non-slip surface. RIGHT: Don't neglect any parts of the dog's coat, taking special care in the sensitive areas.

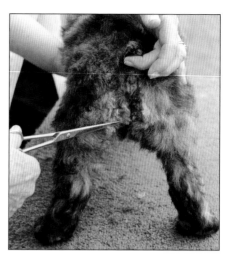

with a heavier growth at the hocks. The hair on the thighs is rather short, not leaving "breeches" on the backside. At the stifle and the hock joints, the length of the hair can be adjusted to accent the angulation. The forelegs should be absolutely straight, round and hairy. Viewed from the front, the elbows may not protrude. The fore- and hindfeet should be trimmed closely and shaped, so as to make them appear beautifully round and compact. The hair between the toes should be cut.

BATHING

You should not bathe your Bouvier more frequently than necessary. It is rare that a Bouvier who has been regularly and properly groomed will need frequent bathing, as the coat naturally tends to repel dirt. You should bathe your Bouvier only when he has become soiled

with dirt or foreign substances not easily removed by brushing. A show Bouvier, however, will be bathed more frequently, as a bath is a necessary part of show preparation. Fortunately, most Bouviers enjoy water and like to swim, so the occasional bath should not present a problem.

When you bathe your dog, remember that soap removes the natural oil from the hair and skin and can cause problems such as skin irritation. A good soap made for dogs and a thorough rinsing to remove residual shampoo are strongly recommended. Your dog should only be bathed after being completely brushed and combed out. This will get rid of most mats and tangles, which are harder to remove when the coat is wet.

Before bathing the dog, have the items you'll need close at hand. First, decide where you will bathe the dog. You should have a tub or basin with a non-slip surface. In warm weather, some like to use a portable pool in the yard, although you'll want to make sure your dog doesn't head for the nearest dirt pile following his bath! You will also need a hose or shower spray to wet the coat thoroughly, a shampoo formulated for dogs, absorbent towels and perhaps a blow dryer. Human shampoos are too harsh for dogs' coats and will dry them out.

Before wetting the dog, give him a brush-through to remove any dead hair, dirt and mats. Make sure he is at ease in the tub and have the water at a comfortable temperature. Begin bathing by wetting the coat all the way down to the skin. Massage in the shampoo, keeping it away from his face and eyes. Rinse him thoroughly, again avoiding the eyes and ears, as you don't want to get water into the ear canals. A thorough rinsing is important, as shampoo residue is drying and itchy to the dog. After rinsing, wrap him in a towel to absorb the initial moisture. You can finish drying with either a towel or a blow dryer on low heat, held at a safe distance from the dog. You should keep the dog indoors and away from drafts until he is completely dry.

NAIL CLIPPING

Having his nails trimmed is not on many dogs' lists of favorite

Examples of successful grooming: TOP: Byou Flora v.d. Vanenblikhoeve, Dutch Champion and winner of many Bests in Show, including the Dutch national specialty. CENTER: Bouvier from the UK, winning at a South Wales Kennel Association show. BOTTOM: Adult Bouvier in a clipped-down "pet" coat.

things to do. With this in mind, you will need to accustom your puppy to the procedure at a young age so that he will sit still (well, as still as he can) for his pedicures. Long nails can cause the dog's feet to spread, which is not good for him; likewise, long nails can hurt if they unintentionally scratch, not good for you!

Some dogs' nails are worn down naturally by regular walking on hard surfaces, so the frequency with which you clip depends on your individual dog. Look at his nails from time to time and clip as needed; a good way to know when it's time for a trim is if you hear your dog clicking as he walks across the floor.

There are several types of nail clippers and even electric nail-grinding tools made for dogs; first we'll discuss using the clipper. To start, have your clipper ready and some doggie treats on hand. You want your pup to view his nail-clipping sessions in a positive light, and what better way to convince him than with food? You may want to enlist the help of an assistant to comfort the pup and offer treats as you concentrate on the clipping itself. The guillotine-type clipper is thought of by many as the easiest type to use; the nail tip is inserted into the opening, and blades on the top and bottom snip it off in one clip.

Start by grasping the pup's paw; a little pressure on the foot

THE EARS KNOW

Cleaning and examining your puppy's ears help ensure good internal health. The ears are the eyes to the dog's innards! Begin handling your puppy's ears when he's still young so that he doesn't protest every time you lift a flap or touch his ears. The ears should be cleaned gently with soft cotton and an ear-cleaning product; *never* probe into the ear or venture farther than you see. Yeast and bacteria are two of the culprits that you can detect by examining the ear. You will notice a strong, often foul, odor, debris, redness or some kind of discharge. All of these point to health problems that can worsen over time. Additionally, you are on the lookout for wax accumulation, ear mites and other tiny bothersome parasites and their even tinier droppings. You may have to pluck hair with tweezers in order to have a better view into the dog's ears, but this is painless if done carefully.

pad causes the nail to extend, making it easier to clip. Clip off a little at a time. If you can see the "quick," which is a blood vessel that runs through each nail, you will know how much to trim, as you do not want to cut into the quick. On that note, if you do cut the quick, which will cause bleeding, you can stem the flow of blood with a styptic pencil or other clotting agent. If you mistakenly nip the quick, do not panic or fuss, as this will cause the pup to be afraid. Simply reassure the pup, stop the bleeding and move on to the next nail. Don't be discouraged; you will become a professional canine pedicurist with practice.

You may or may not be able to see the quick, so it's best to just clip off a small bit at a time. If you see a dark dot in the center of the nail, this is the quick and your cue to stop clipping. Tell the

SCOOTING HIS BOTTOM

Here's a doggy problem that many owners tend to neglect. If your dog is scooting his rear end around the carpet, he probably is experiencing anal-sac impaction or blockage. The anal sacs are the two grape-sized glands on either side of the dog's vent. The dog cannot empty these glands, which become filled with a foul-smelling material. The dog may attempt to lick the area to relieve the pressure. He may also rub his anus on your walls, furniture or floors.

Don't neglect your dog's rear end during grooming sessions. By squeezing both sides of the anus with a soft cloth, you can express some of the material in the sacs. If the material is pasty and thick, you likely will need the assistance of a veterinarian. Vets know how to express the glands and can show you how to do it correctly without hurting the dog or spraying yourself with the contents.

puppy he's a "good boy" and offer a piece of treat with each nail. You can also use nail-clipping time to examine the footpads, making sure that they are not dry and cracked and that nothing has become embedded in them.

The nail grinder, the second choice, is many owners' first choice. Accustoming the puppy to the sound of the grinder and sensation of the buzz presents fewer challenges than the clipper, and there's no chance of cutting through the quick. Use the grinder on a low setting and always talk soothingly to your dog. He won't mind his salon visit, and he'll have nicely polished nails as well.

EYE CARE

During grooming sessions, pay extra attention to the condition of your dog's eyes. If the area around the eyes is soiled or if tear staining has occurred, there are various cleaning agents made especially for this purpose. Look at the dog's eyes to make sure no debris has entered; dogs who spend time outdoors are especially prone to this, but the Bouvier's eyebrows are there to protect his eyes.

The signs of an eye infection are obvious: mucus, redness, puffiness, scabs or other signs of irritation. If your dog's eyes become infected, the vet will likely prescribe an antibiotic ointment for treatment. If you notice signs of more serious problems, such as opacities in the eye, which usually indicate cataracts, consult the vet at once. Taking time to pay attention to your dog's eyes will alert you in the early stages of any problem so that you can get your dog treatment as soon as possible. You could save your dog's sight!

ID FOR YOUR DOG

You love your Bouvier des Flandres and want to keep him safe. Of course you take every precaution to prevent his escaping from the yard or becoming lost or stolen. You have a sturdy high fence and you always keep your dog on lead when out and about in public places. If your dog is not properly identified, however, you are overlooking a major aspect of his safety. We hope to never be in a situation where our dog is missing, but we should practice prevention in the unfortunate case that this happens; identification greatly increases the chances of your dog's being returned to you.

There are several ways to identify your dog. First, the traditional dog tag should be a staple in your dog's wardrobe, attached to his everyday collar. Tags can be made of sturdy plastic and various metals and should include your contact information so that a person who finds the dog can get in touch with you right away to arrange his return. Many people today enjoy the wide range of decorative tags

PET OR STRAY?
Besides the obvious benefit of providing your contact information to whoever finds your lost dog, an ID tag makes your dog more approachable and more likely to be recovered. A strange dog wandering the neighborhood without a collar and tags will look like a stray, while the collar and tags indicate that the dog is someone's pet. Even if the ID tags become detached from the collar, the collar alone will make a person more likely to pick up the dog.

available, so have fun and create a tag to match your dog's personality. Of course, it is important that the tag stays on the collar, so have a secure "O" ring attachment; you also can explore the type of tag that slides right onto the collar.

In addition to the ID tag, which every dog should wear even if identified by another method, two other forms of identification have become popular: microchipping and tattooing. In microchipping, a tiny scannable chip is painlessly inserted under the dog's skin. The number is registered to you so that, if your lost dog turns up at a clinic or shelter, the chip can be scanned to retrieve your contact information.

The advantage of the microchip is that it is a permanent form of ID, but there are some factors to consider. Several different companies make microchips, and not all are compatible with the others' scanning devices. It's best to find a company with a universal microchip that can be read by scanners made by other companies as well. It won't do any good to have the dog chipped if the information cannot be retrieved. Also, not every humane society, shelter and clinic is equipped with a scanner, although more and more facilities are equipping themselves. In fact, many shelters microchip dogs that they adopt out to new homes.

Because the microchip is not visible to the eye, the dog must wear a tag that states that he is microchipped so that whoever picks him up will know to have him scanned. He of course also should have a tag with contact

A large dog needs a large vehicle! An alternative to the travel crate is to partition the back of the vehicle with wire gates to safely confine your dog while traveling.

information in case his chip cannot be read. Humane societies and veterinary clinics offer this service, which is usually very affordable.

Though less popular than microchipping, tattooing is another permanent method of ID for dogs. Most vets perform this service, and there are also clinics that perform dog tattooing. This is also an affordable procedure and one that will not cause much discomfort for the dog. It is best to put the tattoo in a visible area, such as the ear, to deter theft. It is sad to say that there are cases of dogs' being stolen and sold to research laboratories, but such laboratories will not accept tattooed dogs.

To ensure that the tattoo is effective in aiding your dog's return to you, the tattoo number must be registered with a national organization. That way, when someone finds a tattooed dog, a phone call to the registry will quickly match the dog with his owner.

CAR CAUTION

You may like to bring your canine companion along on the daily errands, but if you will be running in and out from place to place and can't bring him indoors with you, leave him at home. Your dog should never be left alone in the car, not even for a minute—never! A car heats up very quickly, and even a cracked-open window will not help. In fact, leaving the window cracked will be dangerous if the dog becomes uncomfortable and tries to escape. When in doubt, leave your dog home, where you know he will be safe.

Simply stated, your Bouvier must be properly trained. Training is the key to molding your dog into a well-behaved companion and canine citizen.

BASIC TRAINING PRINCIPLES: PUPPY VS. ADULT

There's a big difference between training an adult dog and training a young puppy. With a young puppy, everything is new. When he comes home with you, he will be experiencing many things, and he has nothing with which to compare these experiences. Up to this point, he has been with his dam and littermates, not one-on-one with people except in his interactions with his breeder and visitors to the litter.

When you first bring the puppy home, he is eager to please you. This means that he accepts doing things your way. During the next couple of months, he will absorb the basis of everything he needs to know for the rest of his life. This early age is even referred to as the "sponge" stage. After that, for the next 18 months, it's up to you to reinforce good manners by building on the foundation that you've established. Once your puppy is reliable in basic commands and behavior and has reached the appropriate age, you may gradually introduce him

to some of the interesting sports, games and activities available to Bouvier owners and their dogs.

Raising your puppy is a family affair. Each member of the family must know what rules to set forth for the puppy and how to use the same one-word commands to mean exactly the same thing every time. Even if yours is a large family, one person will soon be considered by the pup to be the leader, the Alpha person in his pack, the "boss" who must be obeyed. Often that highly

The young Bouvier is a sponge, ready to absorb everything you teach him. Soak him at an early age!

regarded person turns out to be the one who feeds the puppy. Food ranks very high on the puppy's list of important things! That's why your puppy is rewarded with small treats along with verbal praise when he responds to you correctly. As the puppy learns to do what you want him to do, the food rewards are gradually eliminated and only the praise remains. If you were to keep up with the food treats, you could have two problems on your hands—an obese dog and a beggar.

Training begins the minute your Bouvier des Flandres puppy steps through the doorway of your home, so don't make the mistake of putting the puppy on the floor and telling him by your actions to "Go for it! Run wild!" Even if this is your first puppy, you must act as if you know what you're doing: be the boss. An uncertain pup may be terrified to move, while a bold one will be ready to take you at your word and start plotting to destroy the house! Before you collected your puppy, you decided where his own special place would be, and that's where to put him when you first arrive home. Give him a house tour after he has investigated his area and had a nap and a bathroom "pit stop."

It's worth mentioning here that if you've adopted an adult dog that is completely trained to

your liking, lucky you! You're off the hook! However, if that dog spent his life up to this point in a kennel, or even in a good home but without any real training, be prepared to tackle the job ahead. A dog three years of age or older with no previous training cannot be blamed for not knowing what he was never taught. While the dog is trying to understand and learn your rules, at the same time he has to unlearn many of his previously self-taught habits and general view of the world.

Working with a professional trainer will speed up your progress with an adopted adult

SMILE WHEN YOU ORDER ME AROUND!
While trainers recommend practicing with your dog every day, it's perfectly acceptable to take a "mental health day" off. It's better not to train the dog on days when you're in a sour mood. Your bad attitude or lack of interest will be sensed by your dog and he will respond accordingly. Studies show that dogs are well tuned in to their humans' emotions. Be conscious of how you use your voice when talking to your dog. Raising your voice or shouting will only erode your dog's trust in you as his trainer and master.

dog. You'll need patience, too. Some new rules may be close to impossible for the dog to accept. After all, he's been successful so far by doing everything his way! (Patience again.) He may agree with your instruction for a few days and then slip back into his old ways, so you must be just as consistent and understanding in your teaching as you would be with a puppy. (More patience needed yet again!) Your dog has to learn to pay attention to your voice, your family, the daily routine, new smells, new sounds and, in some cases, even a new climate.

One of the most important things to find out about a newly adopted adult dog is his reaction to children (yours and others), strangers and your friends, and how he acts upon meeting other dogs. If he was not socialized with dogs as a puppy, this could be a major problem. This does not mean that he's a "bad" dog, a vicious dog or an aggressive dog; rather, it means that he has no idea how to read another dog's body language. There's no way for him to tell whether the other dog is a friend or foe. Survival instinct takes over, telling him to attack first and ask questions later. This definitely calls for professional help and, even then, may not be a behavior that can be corrected 100% reliably (or even at all). If you have a puppy, this is why it is

BE UPSTANDING!

You are the dog's leader. During training, stand up straight so your dog looks up at you, and therefore up *to* you. Say the command words distinctly, in a clear, declarative tone of voice. (No barking!) Give rewards only as the correct response takes place (remember your timing!). Praise, smiles and treats are "rewards" used to positively reinforce correct responses. Don't repeat a mistake. Just change to another exercise—you will soon find success!

Once your male Bouvier puppy reaches four months of age, he will discover that it's more fun to aim than squat.

to an outdoor surface as the puppy matures and gains control over his need to eliminate. For the nay-sayers, don't worry—you are training him to go outside, remember? Starting out by paper-training often is the only choice for a city dog, but the Bouvier grows quickly and soon will be too large to "go" on papers.

WHEN YOUR PUPPY'S "GOT TO GO"
Your puppy's need to relieve himself is seemingly non-stop, but signs of improvement will be seen each week. From 8 to 10 weeks old, the puppy will have to be taken outside every time he wakes up, about 10–15 minutes after every meal and after every period of play—all day long, from first

so very important to introduce your young puppy properly to other puppies and "dog-friendly" adult dogs.

HOUSE-TRAINING YOUR BOUVIER DES FLANDRES

Dogs are tactility-oriented when it comes to house-training. In other words, they respond to the surface on which they are given approval to eliminate. The choice is yours (the dog's version is in parentheses): The lawn (including the neighbors' lawns)? A bare patch of earth under a tree (where people like to sit and relax in the summertime)? Concrete steps or patio (all sidewalks, garages and basement floors)? The curbside (watch out for cars)? A small area of crushed stone in a corner of the yard (mine!)? The latter is the best choice if you can manage it, because it will remain strictly for the dog's use and is easy to keep clean.

You can start out with paper-training indoors and switch over

DAILY SCHEDULE
How many relief trips does your puppy need per day? A puppy up to the age of 14 weeks will need to go outside about 8 to 12 times per day! You will have to take the pup out any time he starts sniffing around the floor or turning in small circles, as well as after naps, meals, games and lessons or whenever he's released from his crate. Once the puppy is 14 to 22 weeks of age, he will require only 6 to 8 relief trips. At the ages of 22 to 32 weeks, the puppy will require about 5 to 7 trips. Adult dogs typically require 4 relief trips per day, in the morning, afternoon, evening and late at night.

CANINE DEVELOPMENT SCHEDULE

It is important to understand how and at what age a puppy develops into adulthood. If you are a puppy owner, consult the following Canine Development Schedule to determine the stage of development your puppy is currently experiencing. This knowledge will help you as you work with the puppy in the weeks and months ahead.

PERIOD	AGE	CHARACTERISTICS
FIRST TO THIRD	BIRTH TO SEVEN WEEKS	Puppy needs food, sleep and warmth and responds to simple and gentle touching. Needs mother for security and disciplining. Needs littermates for learning and interacting with other dogs. Pup learns to function within a pack and learns pack order of dominance. Begin socializing pup with adults and children for short periods. Pup begins to become aware of his environment.
FOURTH	EIGHT TO TWELVE WEEKS	Brain is fully developed. Pup needs socializing with outside world. Remove from mother and littermates. Needs to change from canine pack to human pack. Human dominance necessary. Fear period occurs between 8 and 10 weeks. Avoid fright and pain.
FIFTH	THIRTEEN TO SIXTEEN WEEKS	Training and formal obedience should begin. Less association with other dogs, more with people, places, situations. Period will pass easily if you remember this is pup's change-to-adolescence time. Be firm and fair. Flight instinct prominent. Permissiveness and over-disciplining can do permanent damage. Praise for good behavior.
JUVENILE	FOUR TO EIGHT MONTHS	Another fear period about 7 to 8 months of age. It passes quickly, but be cautious of fright and pain. Sexual maturity reached. Dominant traits established. Dog should understand sit, down, come and stay by now.

NOTE: THESE ARE APPROXIMATE TIME FRAMES. ALLOW FOR INDIVIDUAL DIFFERENCES IN PUPPIES.

thing in the morning until his bedtime! That's a total of ten or more trips per day to teach the puppy where it's okay to relieve himself. With that schedule in mind, you can see that house-training a young puppy is not a part-time job. It requires someone to be home all day.

If that seems overwhelming or impossible, do a little planning. For example, plan to pick up your puppy at the start of a vacation period. If you can't get home in the middle of the day, plan to hire a dog-sitter or ask a neighbor to come over to take the pup outside, feed him his lunch and then take him out again about ten or so minutes after he's eaten. Also make arrangements with that or another person to be your "emergency" contact if you have to stay late on the job. Remind yourself—repeatedly—that this hectic schedule improves as the puppy gets older.

HOME WITHIN A HOME

Your Bouvier des Flandres puppy needs to be confined to one secure, puppy-proof area when no one is able to watch his every move. Generally the kitchen is the place of choice because the floor is washable. Likewise, it's a busy family area that will accustom the pup to a variety of noises, everything from pots and pans to the telephone, blender and dishwasher. He will also be enchanted by the smell of your cooking (and will never be critical when you burn something). An exercise pen (also called an "ex-pen," a puppy version of a playpen) within the room of choice is an excellent means of confinement for a young pup. He can see out and has a certain amount of space in which to run about, but he is safe from dangerous things like electrical cords, heating units, trash baskets or open kitchen-supply cabinets. Place the pen where the puppy will not get a blast of heat or air conditioning.

LEASH TRAINING

House-training and leash training go hand in hand, literally. When taking your puppy outside to do his business, lead him there on his leash. Unless an emergency potty run is called for, do not whisk the puppy up into your arms and take him outside. If you have a fenced yard, you have the advantage of letting the puppy loose to go out, but it's better to put the dog on the leash and take him to his designated place in the yard until he is reliably house-trained. Taking the puppy for a walk is the best way to house-train a dog. The dog will associate the walk with his time to relieve himself, and the exercise of walking stimulates the dog's bowels and bladder. Dogs that are not trained to relieve themselves on a walk may hold it until they get back home, which of course defeats half the purpose of the walk.

Your Bouvier puppy must always be under your control and supervision, both for setting the rules of the house and for his safety.

In the pen, you can put a few toys, his bed (which can be his crate if the dimensions of pen and crate are compatible) and a few layers of newspaper in one small corner, just in case. A water bowl can be hung at a convenient height on the side of the ex-pen so it won't become a splashing pool for an innovative puppy. His food dish can go on the floor, near but not under the water bowl.

Crates are something that pet owners are at last getting used to for their dogs. Wild or domestic canines have always preferred to sleep in den-like safe spots, and that is exactly what the crate provides. How often have you seen adult dogs that choose to sleep under a table or chair even though they have full run of the house? It's the den connection.

In your "happy" voice, use the word "Crate" every time you put the pup into his den. If he's new to a crate, toss in a small biscuit for him to chase the first few times. At night, after he's been outside, he should sleep in his crate. The crate may be kept in his designated area at night or, if you want to be sure to hear those wake-up yips in the morning, put the crate in a corner of your bedroom. However, don't make any response whatsoever to whining or crying. If he's completely ignored, he'll settle down and get to sleep.

Good bedding for a young puppy is an old folded bath towel

parts, bits of stuffing or plastic or any other small pieces can cause intestinal blockage or possibly choking if swallowed.

PROGRESSING WITH POTTY-TRAINING
After you've taken your puppy out and he has relieved himself in the area you've selected, he can have some free time with the family as long as there is some-

Going out is half the battle—there's the "coming back in" part too!

or an old blanket, something that is easily washable and disposable if necessary ("accidents" will happen!). Never put newspaper in the puppy's crate. Also, those old ideas about adding a clock to replace his mother's heartbeat, or a hot-water bottle to replace her warmth, are just that—old ideas. The clock could drive the puppy nuts, and the hot-water bottle could end up as a very soggy waterbed! An extremely good breeder would have introduced your puppy to the crate by letting two pups sleep together for a couple of nights, followed by several nights alone. How thankful you will be if you found that breeder!

Safe toys in the pup's crate or area will keep him occupied, but monitor their condition closely. Discard any toys that show signs of being chewed to bits. Squeaky

SOMEBODY TO BLAME
House-training a puppy can be frustrating for the puppy and the owner alike. The puppy does not instinctively understand the difference between defecating on the pavement outside and on the ceramic tile in the kitchen. He is confused and frightened by his human's exuberant reactions to his natural urges. The owner, arguably the more intelligent of the duo, is also frustrated that he cannot convince his puppy to obey his commands and instructions.

In frustration, the owner may struggle with the temptation to discipline the puppy, scold him or even strike him on the rear end. Harsh corrections are not only inappropriate but also will defeat your purpose in gaining your puppy's trust and respect. Don't blame your nine-week-old puppy. Blame yourself for not being 100% consistent in the puppy's lessons and routine. The lesson here is simple: try harder and your puppy will succeed.

one responsible for watching him. That doesn't mean just someone in the same room who is watching TV or busy on the computer, but one person who is doing nothing other than keeping an eye on the pup, playing with him on the floor and helping him understand his position in the pack.

This first taste of freedom will let you begin to set the house rules. If you don't want the dog on the furniture, now is the time to prevent his first attempts to jump up onto the couch. The word to use in this case is "Off," not "Down." "Down" is the word you will use to teach the down position, which is something entirely different.

Most corrections at this stage come in the form of simply distracting the puppy. Instead of telling him "No" for "Don't chew the carpet," distract the chomping puppy with a toy and he'll forget about the carpet.

As you are playing with the pup, do not forget to watch him closely and pay attention to his body language. Whenever you see him begin to circle or sniff, take the puppy outside to relieve himself. Praise him as he eliminates while he actually is in the act of relieving himself. Three seconds after he has finished is too late! You'll be praising him for running toward you, or picking up a toy or whatever he may be doing at that moment, and that's not what you want to be praising him for. Timing is a vital tool in all dog training. Use it.

Scent attraction is why it's so important to clean up any messes made in the house by using a product specially made to eliminate the odor of dog urine and droppings. Regular household cleansers won't do the trick. Pet shops sell the best pet deodorizers. Invest in the largest container you can find.

Scent attraction eventually will lead your pup to his chosen spot outdoors; this is the basis of outdoor training. When you take your puppy outside to relieve himself, use a one-word command such as "Outside" or "Go-potty" (that's one word to the puppy!) as you pick him up and attach his leash. Then put him down in his area. If for any reason you can't carry him, snap the leash on quickly and lead him to his spot.

The nose knows! Scent attraction is how the pup learns to locate his chosen relief area once he's used it.

TIPS FOR
TRAINING AND SAFETY

1. Whether on- or off-leash, practice only in a fenced area.
2. Remove the training collar when the training session is over.
3. Don't try to break up a dogfight.
4. "Come," "Leave it" and "Wait" are safety commands.
5. The dog belongs in a crate or behind a barrier when riding in the car.
6. Don't ignore the dog's first sign of aggression. Aggression only gets worse, so take it seriously.
7. Keep the faces of children and dogs separated.
8. Pay attention to what the dog is chewing.
9. Keep the vet's number near your phone.
10. "Okay" is a useful release command.

Now comes the hard part—hard for you, that is. Just stand there until he urinates and defecates. Move him a few feet in one direction or another if he's just sitting there looking at you, but remember that this is neither playtime nor time for a walk. This is strictly a business trip! Then, as he circles and squats (remember your timing!), give him a quiet "Good dog" as praise. If you start to jump for joy, ecstatic over his performance, he'll do one of two things: either he will stop mid-stream, as it were, or he'll do it

again for you—in the house—and expect you to be just as delighted!

Give him five minutes or so and, if he doesn't go in that time, take him back indoors to his confined area and try again in another ten minutes, or immediately if you see him sniffing and circling. By careful observation, you'll soon work out a successful schedule.

Accidents, by the way, are just that—accidents. Clean them up quickly and thoroughly, without comment, after the puppy has been taken outside to finish his business and then put back into his area or crate. If you witness an accident in progress, say "No!" in a stern voice and get the pup outdoors immediately. No punishment is needed. You and your puppy are just learning each other's language, and sometimes it's easy to miss a puppy's message. Chalk it up to experience and watch more closely from now on.

KEEPING THE PACK ORDERLY
Discipline is a form of training that brings order to life. For example, military discipline is what allows the soldiers in an army to work as one. Discipline is a form of teaching and, in dogs, is the basis of how the successful pack operates. Each member knows his place in the pack and all respect the leader, or Alpha dog. It is essential for your puppy that you establish this type of relationship,

with you as the Alpha, or leader. It is a form of social coexistence that all canines recognize and accept. Discipline, therefore, is never to be confused with punishment. When you teach your puppy how you want him to behave, and he behaves properly and you praise him for it, you are disciplining him with a form of positive reinforcement.

For a dog, rewards come in the form of praise, a smile, a cheerful tone of voice, a few friendly pats or a rub of the ears. Rewards are also small food treats. Obviously, that does not mean bits of regular dog food. Instead, treats are very small bits of special things like cheese or pieces of soft

WHO'S TRAINING WHOM?

Dog training is a black-and-white exercise. The correct response to a command must be absolute, and the trainer must insist on completely accurate responses from the dog. A trainer cannot command his dog to sit and then settle for the dog's melting into the down position. Often owners are so pleased that their dogs "did something" in response to a command that they just shrug and say, "OK, Down" even though they wanted the dog to sit. You want your dog to respond to the command without hesitation: he must respond at that moment and correctly every time.

dog treats. The idea is to reward the dog with something very small that he can taste and swallow, providing instant positive reinforcement. If he has to take time to chew the treat, by the time he is finished he will have forgotten what he did to earn it!

Your puppy should never be physically punished. The displeasure shown on your face and in your voice is sufficient to signal to the pup that he has done something wrong. He wants to please everyone higher up on the social ladder, especially his leader, so a scowl and harsh voice will take care of the error.

Dogs respond much better to affection and praise than to punishment. Training using positive reinforcement builds a bond of friendship between human teacher and canine student.

Growling out the word "Shame!" when the pup is caught in the act of doing something wrong is better than the repetitive "No." Some dogs hear "No" so often that they begin to think it's their name! By the way, do not use the dog's name when you're correcting him. His name is reserved to get his attention for something pleasant about to take place.

There are punishments that have nothing to do with you. For example, your dog may think that chasing cats is one reason for his existence. You can try to stop it as much as you like but without success, because it's such fun for the dog. But one good hissing, spitting, swipe of a cat's claws across the dog's nose will put an end to the game forever. Intervene only when your dog's eyeball is seriously at risk. Cat scratches can cause permanent damage to an innocent but annoying puppy.

PUPPY KINDERGARTEN

COLLAR AND LEASH
Before you begin your Bouvier des Flandres puppy's education, he must be used to his collar and leash. Choose a collar for your puppy that is secure, but not heavy or bulky. He won't enjoy training if he's uncomfortable. A flat buckle collar is fine for every-day wear and for initial puppy training. For older dogs, there are several types of training collars

such as the martingale, which is a double loop that tightens slightly around the neck, or the head collar, which is similar to a horse's halter. Do not use a chain choke collar unless you have been specifically shown how to put it on and how to use it. You may not be disposed to use a chain choke collar even if your breeder has told you that it's suitable for your Bouvier des Flandres.

A lightweight 6-foot woven cotton or nylon training leash is preferred by most trainers because it is easy to fold up in your hand and comfortable to hold because there is a certain amount of give to it. There are lessons where the dog will start off 6 feet away from you at the end of the leash. The leash used to take the puppy outside to relieve himself is shorter because you don't want him to roam away from his area. The shorter leash will also be the one to use when you walk the puppy.

If you've been wise enough to enroll in a Puppy Kindergarten training class, suggestions will be

"SCHOOL" MODE
When is your puppy ready for a lesson? Maybe not always when you are. Attempting training with treats just before his mealtime is asking for disaster. Notice what times of day he performs best and make that Fido's school time.

made as to the best collar and leash for your young puppy. I say "wise" because your puppy will be in a class with puppies in his age range (up to five months old) of all breeds and sizes. It's the perfect way for him to learn the right way (and the wrong way) to interact with other dogs as well as their people. You cannot teach your puppy how to interpret another dog's sign language. For a first-time puppy owner, these socialization classes are invaluable. For experienced dog owners, they are a real boon to further training.

ATTENTION

You've been using the dog's name since the minute you collected him from the breeder, so you should be able to get his attention by saying his name—with a big smile and in an excited tone of voice. His response will be the puppy equivalent of "Here I am! What are we going to do?" Your immediate response (if you haven't guessed by now) is "Good dog." Rewarding him at the moment he pays attention to you teaches him the proper way to respond when he hears his name.

EXERCISES FOR A BASIC CANINE EDUCATION

THE SIT EXERCISE

There are several ways to teach the puppy to sit. The first one is to catch him whenever he is about

to sit and, as his backside nears the floor, say "Sit, good dog!" That's positive reinforcement and, if your timing is sharp, he will learn that what he's doing at that second is connected to your saying "Sit" and that you think he's clever for doing it!

READY, SIT, GO!

On your marks, get set: train! Most professional trainers agree that the sit command is the place to start your dog's formal education. Sitting is a natural posture for most dogs, and they respond to the sit exercise willingly and readily. For every lesson, begin with the sit command so that you start out on a successful note; likewise, you should practice the sit command at the end of every lesson as well, because you always want to end on a high note.

verbal command and the motion of the hand are signals for the sit. Your puppy is watching you almost more than he is listening to you, so what you do is just as important as what you say.

Don't save any of these drills only for training sessions. Use them as much as possible at odd times during a normal day. The dog should always sit before being given his food dish. He should sit to let you go through a doorway first, when the doorbell rings or when you stop to speak to someone on the street.

THE DOWN EXERCISE

Before beginning to teach the down command, you must consider how the dog feels about this exercise. To him, "Down" is a submissive position. Being flat on

The down requires a little more persistence to teach than the sit, but your Bouvier will comply if you take a positive approach.

Another method is to start with the puppy on his leash in front of you. Show him a treat in the palm of your right hand. Bring your hand up under his nose and, almost in slow motion, move your hand up and back so his nose goes up in the air and his head tilts back as he follows the treat in your hand. At that point, he will have to either sit or fall over, so as his back legs buckle under, say "Sit, good dog," and then give him the treat and lots of praise. You may have to begin with your hand lightly running up his chest, actually lifting his chin up until he sits. Some (usually older) dogs require gentle pressure on their hindquarters with the left hand, in which case the dog should be on your left side. Puppies generally do not appreciate this physical dominance.

After a few times, you should be able to show the dog a treat in the open palm of your hand, raise your hand waist-high as you say "Sit" and have him sit. You thereby will have taught him two things at the same time. Both the

> **BASIC PRINCIPLES OF DOG TRAINING**
> 1. Start training early. A young puppy is ready, willing and able.
> 2. Timing is your all-important tool. Praise at the exact time that the dog responds correctly. Pay close attention.
> 3. Patience is almost as important as timing!
> 4. Repeat! The same word has to mean the same thing every time.
> 5. In the beginning, praise all correct behavior verbally, along with treats and petting.

OKAY!

This is the signal that tells your dog that he can quit whatever he was doing. Use "Okay" to end a session on a correct response to a command. (Never end on an incorrect response.) Lots of praise follows. People use "Okay" a lot and it has other uses for dogs, too. Your dog is barking. You say, "Okay! Come!" "Okay" signals him to stop the barking activity and "Come" allows him to come to you for a "Good dog."

the floor with you standing over him is not his idea of fun. It's up to you to let him know that, while it may not be fun, the reward of your approval is worth his effort.

Start with the puppy on your left side in a sit position. Hold the leash right above his collar in your left hand. Have an extra-special treat, such as a small piece of cooked chicken or hot dog, in your right hand. Place it at the end of the pup's nose and steadily move your hand down and forward along the ground. Hold the leash to prevent a sudden lunge for the food. As the puppy goes into the down position, say "Down" very gently.

The difficulty with this exercise is twofold: it's both the submissive aspect and the fact that most people say the word "Down" as if they were a drill sergeant in charge of recruits! So issue the command sweetly, give him the treat and have the pup maintain the down position for several seconds. If he tries to get up immediately, place your hands on his shoulders and press down gently, giving him a very quiet "Good dog." As you progress with this lesson, increase the "down time" until he will hold it until you say "Okay" (his cue for release). Practice this one in the house at various times throughout the day.

By increasing the length of time during which the dog must maintain the down position, you'll find many uses for it. For example, he can lie at your feet in the vet's office or anywhere that both of you have to wait, when you are on the phone, while the family is eating and so forth. If you progress to training for competitive obedience, he'll already be all set for the exercise called the "long down."

Only use a chain collar as a training collar if you know exactly how to use it. There are many types of training collars to choose from.

Increase the length of the sit/stay each time until the dog can hold it for at least 30 seconds without moving. After about a week of success, move out on your right foot and take two steps before turning to face the dog. Give the "Stay" hand signal (left palm back toward the dog's head) as you leave. He gets the treat when you return and he holds the sit/stay. Increase the distance that you walk away from him before turning until you reach the length of your training leash. But don't rush it! Go back to the beginning if he moves before he should. No matter what the lesson, never be upset by having to back up for a few days. The repetition and practice are what will make your dog reliable in these commands. It won't do any good to move on to something more difficult if the command is not mastered at the

Start teaching "stay" with the dog on lead, using both verbal and hand signals. Progress to off-lead training only in a secure area and only after the dog is reliable with the command on lead.

THE STAY EXERCISE

You can teach your Bouvier des Flandres to stay in the sit, down and stand positions. To teach the sit/stay, have the dog sit on your left side. Hold the leash at waist level in your left hand and let the dog know that you have a treat in your closed right hand. Step forward on your right foot as you say "Stay." Immediately turn and stand directly in front of the dog, keeping your right hand up high so he'll keep his eye on the treat hand and maintain the sit position for a count of five. Return to your original position and offer the reward.

BOOT CAMP

Even if one member of the family assumes the role of "drill sergeant," every other member of the family has to know what's involved in the dog's education. Success depends on consistency and knowing what words to use, how to use them, how to say them, when to say them and most important to the dog, how to praise. The dog will be happy to respond to all members of the family, but don't make the little guy think he's in boot camp!

easier levels. Above all, even if you do get frustrated, never let your puppy know! Always keep a positive, upbeat attitude during training, which will transmit to your dog for positive results.

The down/stay is taught in the same way once the dog is completely reliable and steady with the down command. Again, don't rush it. With the dog in the down position on your left side, step out on your right foot as you say "Stay." Return by walking around in back of the dog and into your original position. While you are training, it's okay to murmur something like "Hold on" to encourage him to stay put. When the dog will stay without moving when you are at a distance of 3 or 4 feet, begin to increase the length of time before you return. Be sure he holds the down on your return until you say "Okay." At that point, he gets his treat—just so he'll remember for next time that it's not over until it's over.

THE COME EXERCISE

No command is more important to the safety of your Bouvier des Flandres than "Come." It is what you should say every single time you see the puppy running toward you: "Binky, come! Good dog." During playtime, run a few feet away from the puppy and turn and tell him to "Come" as he is already running to you. You can go so far

> ### SHOULD WE ENROLL?
> If you have the means and the time, you should definitely take your dog to obedience classes. Begin with Puppy Kindergarten classes in which puppies of all sizes learn basic lessons while getting the opportunity to meet and greet each other; it's as much about socialization as it is about good manners. What you learn in class you can practice at home. And if you goof up in practice, you'll get help in the next session.

as to teach your puppy two things at once if you squat down and hold out your arms. As the pup gets close to you and you're saying "Good dog," bring your right arm in about waist high. Now he's also learning the hand signal, an excellent device should you be on the phone when you need to get him to come to you. You'll also both be one step ahead when you enter obedience classes.

When the puppy responds to your well-timed "Come," try it with the puppy on the training leash. This time, catch him off guard, while he's sniffing a leaf or watching a bird: "Binky, come!" You may have to pause for a split second after his name to be sure you have his attention. If the puppy shows any sign of confusion, give the leash a mild jerk and take a couple of steps backward. Do not repeat the

COME AND GET IT!
The come command is your dog's safety signal. Until he is 99% perfect in responding, don't use the come command if you cannot enforce it. Practice on leash with treats or squeakers, or whenever the dog is running to you. Never call him to come to you if he is to be corrected for a misdemeanor. Reward the dog with a treat and happy praise whenever he comes to you.

command. In this case, you should say "Good come" as he reaches you.

That's the number-one rule of training. Each command word is given just once. Anything more is nagging. You'll also notice that all commands are one word only. Even when they are actually two words, you say them as one.

Never call the dog to come to you—with or without his name—if you are angry or intend to correct him for some misbehavior. When correcting the pup, you go to him. Your dog must always connect "Come" with something pleasant and with your approval; then you can rely on his response.

Puppies, like children, have notoriously short attention spans, so don't overdo it with any of the training. Keep each lesson short. Break it up with a quick run

Running eagerly to you is how you want your puppy to respond to your call.

around the yard or a ball toss, repeat the lesson and quit as soon as the pup gets it right. That way, you will always end with a "Good dog."

Life isn't perfect and neither are puppies. A time will come, often around ten months of age, when he'll become "selectively deaf" or choose to "forget" his name. He may respond by wagging his tail (and even seeming to smile at you) with a look that says "Make me!" Laugh, throw his favorite toy and skip the lesson you had planned. Pups will be pups!

THE HEEL EXERCISE

The second most important command to teach, after the come, is the heel. When you are walking your growing puppy, you need to be in control. Besides, it looks terrible to be pulled and yanked down the street, and it's not much fun either. Imagine trying to

control an untrained adult Bouvier! Your eight-week-old puppy will probably follow you everywhere, but that's his natural instinct, not your control over the situation. However, any time he does follow you, you can say "Heel" and be ahead of the game, as he will learn to associate this command with the action of following you before you even begin teaching him to heel.

There is a very precise, almost military, procedure for teaching your dog to heel. As with all other obedience training, begin with the dog on your left side. He will be in a very nice sit and you will have the training leash across your chest. Hold the loop and folded leash in your right hand. Pick up the slack leash above the dog in your left hand and hold it loosely at your side. Step out on your left foot as you say "Heel." If the puppy does not move, give a gentle tug or pat your left leg to get him started. If he surges ahead of you, stop and pull him back gently until he is at your side. Tell him to sit and begin again.

Walk a few steps and stop while the puppy is correctly beside you. Tell him to sit and give mild verbal praise. (More enthusiastic praise will encourage him to think the lesson is over.) Repeat the lesson, increasing the number of steps you take only as long as the dog is heeling nicely beside you. When you end the

lesson, have him hold the sit and then give him the "Okay" to let him know that this is the end of the lesson. Praise him so that he knows he did a good job.

The cure for excessive pulling

LET'S GO!
Many people use "Let's go" instead of "Heel" when teaching their dogs to behave on lead. It sounds more like fun! When beginning to teach the heel, whatever command you use, always step off on your left foot. That's the one next to the dog, who is on your left side, in case you've forgotten. Keep a loose leash. When the dog pulls ahead, stop, bring him back and begin again. Use treats to guide him around turns.

(a common problem) is to stop when the dog is no more than 2 or 3 feet ahead of you. Guide him back into position and begin again. With a really determined puller, try switching to a head collar. This will automatically turn the pup's head toward you so you can bring him back easily to the heel position. Give quiet, reassuring praise every time the leash goes slack and he's staying with you.

Staying and heeling can take a lot out of a dog, so provide playtime and free-running exercise to shake off the stress when the lessons are over. You don't want him to associate training with all work and no fun.

At home on the farm, the Bouvier will love opportunities to develop his instinctive abilities.

OBEDIENCE CLASSES

The advantages of an obedience class are that your dog will have to learn amid the distractions of other people and dogs and that your mistakes will be quickly corrected by the trainer. Teaching your dog along with a qualified instructor and other handlers who may have more dog experience than you is another plus of the class environment. The instructor and other handlers can help you to find the most efficient way of teaching your dog a command or exercise. It's often easier to learn by other people's mistakes than your own. You will also learn all of the requirements for competitive obedience trials, in which you can earn titles and go on to advanced jumping and retrieving exercises, which are fun for many dogs. Obedience classes build the foundation needed for many other canine activities.

TRAINING FOR OTHER ACTIVITIES

Once your dog has basic obedience under his collar and is 12 months of age, you can enter the world of agility training. Dogs think agility is pure fun, like being turned loose in an amusement park full of obstacles! In addition to agility, the Bouvier can participate in herding trials and tracking, which is open to all "nosey" dogs (which would include all dogs!). For those who

NO MORE TREATS!

When your dog is responding promptly and correctly to commands, it's time to eliminate treats. Begin by alternating a treat reward with a verbal-praise-only reward. Gradually eliminate all treats while increasing the frequency of praise. Overlook pleading eyes and expectant expressions, but if he's still watching your treat hand, you're on your way to using hand signals.

have the opportunity to participate in Schutzhund with your Bouvier if you choose. Schutzhund originated as a test to determine the best quality dogs to be used for breeding stock. Breeders continue to use it as a way to evaluate working ability and temperament. Each level consists of training, obedience and protection phases. Training for Schutzhund is intense, should be done with an experienced trainer and must be practiced consistently to keep the dog keen.

Around the house, your Bouvier des Flandres can be taught to do some simple chores. You might teach him to carry a basket of household items or to fetch the morning newspaper. The kids can teach the dog all kinds of tricks, from playing hide-and-seek to balancing a biscuit on his nose. A family dog is what rounds out the family. Everything he does, whether activities or just gazing lovingly at you, represents the bonus of owning a dog.

Don't forget to play! What better reward for a lesson learned than a game of fetch with his favorite teacher and playmate... you!

like to volunteer, there is the wonderful feeling of owning a therapy dog and visiting hospices, nursing homes and veterans' homes to bring smiles, comfort and companionship to those who live there.

In some countries, you will

HEALTHCARE OF YOUR

BOUVIER DES FLANDRES

By Lowell Ackerman DVM, DACVD

HEALTHCARE FOR A LIFETIME
When you own a dog, you become his healthcare advocate over his entire lifespan, as well as being the one to shoulder the financial burden of such care. Accordingly, it is worthwhile to focus on prevention rather than treatment, as you and your pet will both be happier.

Regarding healthcare issues specifically, it is very difficult to make blanket statements about where to acquire a problem-free pet, but, again, a reputable breeder is your best bet. In an ideal situation, you have the opportunity to see both parents, get references from other owners of the breeder's pups and see genetic-testing documentation for several generations of the litter's ancestors. At the very least, you must thoroughly investigate the Bouvier des Flandres and the problems inherent in that breed, as well as the genetic testing available to screen for those problems. We've also discussed that evaluating the behavioral nature of your Bouvier des Flandres and that of his immediate family members is an important part of the selection process that cannot be underestimated or overemphasized.

Assuming that you have started off with a pup from healthy, sound stock, you then become responsible for helping your veterinarian keep your pet healthy. Some crucial things happen before you even bring your puppy home. Parasite control typically begins at two weeks of age, and vaccinations typically begin at six to eight weeks of age. A pre-pubertal evaluation is typically scheduled for about six months of age. At this time, a dental evaluation is done (since the adult teeth are now in), heartworm prevention is started and neutering or spaying is most commonly done.

It is critical to commence regular dental care at home if you have not already done so. It may not sound very important, but most dogs have active periodontal disease by four years of age if they don't have their teeth cleaned regularly at home, not just at their veterinary exams. Dental problems lead to more than just bad "doggie breath." Gum disease can have very serious medical consequences. If you start brushing your dog's teeth and using antiseptic rinses from a young age, your dog will be accustomed to it and will not resist. The results will be healthy dentition, which your pet will need to enjoy a long, healthy life.

Most dogs are considered adults at a year of age, although some larger breeds still have some filling out to do up to about two or so years old. Even individual dogs within each breed have different healthcare requirements, so work with your veterinarian to determine what will be needed and what your role should be. This doctor-client relationship is important, because as vaccination guidelines change, there may not be an annual "vaccine visit" scheduled. You must make sure that you see your veterinarian at least annually, even if no vaccines are due, because this is the best opportunity to coordinate healthcare activities and to make sure that no medical issues creep by unaddressed.

When your Bouvier des Flandres reaches three-quarters of his anticipated lifespan, he is considered a "senior" and likely requires some special care. In general, if you've been taking great care of your canine companion throughout his formative and adult years, the transition to

Tail docking, when performed, is done by the vet when the pup is only a few days old.

senior status should be a smooth one. Age is not a disease, and as long as everything is functioning as it should, there is no reason why most of late adulthood should not be rewarding for both you and your pet. This is especially true if you have tended to the details, such as regular veterinary visits, proper dental care, excellent nutrition and management of bone and joint issues.

At the senior stage in your Bouvier des Flandres's life, your veterinarian may want to schedule visits twice yearly, instead of once, to run some laboratory screenings, electrocardiograms and the like, and to change the diet to something more digestible. Catching problems early is the best way to manage them effectively. Treating the early stages of heart disease is so much easier than trying to intervene when there is more significant damage to the heart muscle. Similarly, managing the beginning of kidney problems is fairly routine if there is no significant kidney damage. Other problems, like cognitive dysfunction (similar to senility and Alzheimer's disease), cancer, diabetes and arthritis, are more common in older dogs, but all can be treated to help the dog live as many happy, comfortable years as possible. Just as in people, medical management is more effective (and less expensive) when you catch things early.

SELECTING A VETERINARIAN

There is probably no more important decision that you will make regarding your pet's healthcare than the selection of his doctor. Your pet's veterinarian will be a pediatrician, family-practice

Still looking like a youngster, this healthy, hardy Bouvier is a "senior citizen" of 12 years of age.

physician and gerontologist, depending on the dog's life stage, and will be the individual who makes recommendations regarding issues such as when specialists need to be consulted, when diagnostic testing and/or therapeutic intervention is needed and when you will need to seek outside emergency and critical-care services. Your vet will act as your advocate and liaison throughout these processes.

Everyone has his own idea about what to look for in a vet, an individual who will play a big role in his dog's (and, of course, his own) life for many years to come. For some, it is the compassionate caregiver with whom they hope to develop a professional relationship to span the lifetime of their dogs and even their future pets. For others, they are seeking a clinician with keen diagnostic and therapeutic insight who can deliver state-of-the-art healthcare. Still others need a veterinary facility that is open evenings and weekends, or is in close proximity or provides mobile veterinary services, to accommodate their schedules; these people may not much mind that their dogs might see different veterinarians on each visit. Just as we have different reasons for selecting our own healthcare professionals (e.g., covered by insurance plan, expert in field, convenient location, etc.), we should not expect that there is a one-size-fits-all recommendation for selecting a veterinarian and veterinary practice. The best advice is to be honest in your assessment of what you expect from a veterinary practice and to conscientiously research the options in your area. You will quickly appreciate that not all veterinary practices are the same, and you will be happiest with one that truly meets your needs.

There is another point to be considered in the selection of veterinary services. Not that long ago, a single veterinarian would attempt to manage all medical and surgical issues as they arose. That was often problematic, because veterinarians are trained in many species and many diseases, and it was just impossible for general veterinary practitioners to be experts in every species, every field and every ailment. However, just as in the human healthcare fields, specialization has allowed general practitioners to concentrate on primary healthcare delivery, especially wellness and the prevention of infectious diseases, and to utilize a network of specialists to assist in the management of conditions that require specific expertise and experience. Thus there are now many types of veterinary specialists, including dermatologists, cardiologists, ophthalmologists, surgeons, internists, oncologists, neurologists, behaviorists, criticalists and others to help

YOUR DOG NEEDS TO VISIT THE VET IF:

- He has ingested a toxin such as antifreeze or a toxic plant; in these cases, administer first aid and call the vet right away
- His teeth are discolored, loose or missing or he has sores or other signs of infection or abnormality in the mouth
- He has been vomiting, has had diarrhea or has been constipated for over 24 hours; call immediately if you notice blood
- He has refused food for over 24 hours
- His eating habits, water intake or toilet habits have noticeably changed; if you have noticed weight gain or weight loss
- He shows symptoms of bloat, which requires immediate attention
- He is salivating excessively
- He has a lump in his throat
- He has a lump or bumps anywhere on the body
- He is very lethargic
- He appears to be in pain or otherwise has trouble chewing or swallowing
- His skin loses elasticity

Of course, there will be other instances in which a visit to the vet is necessary; these are just some of the signs that could be indicative of serious problems that need to be caught as early as possible.

primary-care veterinarians deal with complicated medical challenges. In most cases, specialists see cases referred by primary-care veterinarians, make diagnoses and set up management plans. From there, the animals' ongoing care is returned to their primary-care veterinarians. This important team approach to your pet's medical-care needs has provided opportunities for advanced care and an unparalleled level of quality to be delivered.

With all of the opportunities for your Bouvier des Flandres to receive high-quality veterinary medical care, there is another topic that needs to be addressed at the same time—cost. It's been said that you can have excellent healthcare or inexpensive healthcare, but never both; this is as true in veterinary medicine as it is in human medicine. While veterinary costs are a fraction of what the same services cost in the human healthcare arena, it is still difficult to deal with unanticipated medical costs, especially since they can easily creep into hundreds or even thousands of dollars if specialists or emergency services become involved. However, there are ways of managing these risks. The easiest is to buy pet health insurance and realize that its foremost purpose is not to cover routine healthcare visits but rather to serve as an umbrella for those rainy days

when your pet needs medical care and you don't want to worry about whether or not you can afford that care.

VACCINATIONS AND INFECTIOUS DISEASES

There has never been an easier time to prevent a variety of infectious diseases in your dog, but the advances we've made in veterinary medicine come with a price—choice. Now while it may seem that choice is a good thing (and it is), it has never been more difficult for the pet owner (or the veterinarian) to make an informed

PET INSURANCE

Pet insurance policies are very cost-effective (and very inexpensive by human health-insurance standards), but make sure that you buy the policy long before you intend to use it (preferably starting in puppyhood, because coverage will exclude pre-existing conditions) and that you are actually buying an indemnity insurance plan from an insurance company that is regulated by your state or province. Many insurance policy look-alikes are actually discount clubs that are redeemable only at specific locations and for specific services. An indemnity plan covers your pet at almost all veterinary, specialty and emergency practices and is an excellent way to manage your pet's ongoing healthcare needs.

COMMON INFECTIOUS DISEASES

Let's discuss some of the diseases that create the need for vaccination in the first place. Following are the major canine infectious diseases and a simple explanation of each.

Rabies: A devastating viral disease that can be fatal in dogs and people. In fact, vaccination of dogs and cats is an important public-health measure to create a resistant animal buffer population to protect people from contracting the disease. Vaccination schedules are determined on a government level and are not optional for pet owners; rabies vaccination is required by law in all 50 states.

Parvovirus: A severe, potentially life-threatening disease that is easily transmitted between dogs. There are four strains of the virus, but it is believed that there is significant "cross-protection" between strains that may be included in individual vaccines.

Distemper: A potentially severe and life-threatening disease with a relatively high risk of exposure, especially in certain regions. In very high-risk distemper environments, young pups may be vaccinated with human measles vaccine, a related virus that offers cross-protection when administered at four to ten weeks of age.

Hepatitis: Caused by canine adenovirus type 1 (CAV-1), but since vaccination with the causative virus has a higher rate of adverse effects, cross-protection is derived from the use of adenovirus type 2 (CAV-2), a cause of respiratory disease and one of the potential causes of canine cough. Vaccination with CAV-2 provides long-term immunity against hepatitis, but relatively less protection against respiratory infection.

Canine cough: Also called tracheobronchitis, actually a fairly complicated result of viral and bacterial offenders; therefore, even with vaccination, protection is incomplete. Wherever dogs congregate, canine cough will likely be spread among them. Intranasal vaccination with *Bordetella* and parainfluenza is the best safeguard, but the duration of immunity does not appear to be very long, typically a year at most. These are non-core vaccines, but vaccination is sometimes mandated by boarding kennels, obedience classes, dog shows and other places where dogs congregate to try to minimize spread of infection.

Leptospirosis: A potentially fatal disease that is more common in some geographic regions. It is capable of being spread to humans. The disease varies with the individual "serovar," or strain, of *Leptospira* involved. Since there does not appear to be much cross-protection between serovars, protection is only as good as the likelihood that the serovar in the vaccine is the same as the one in the pet's local environment. Problems with *Leptospira* vaccines are that protection does not last very long, side effects are not uncommon and a large percentage of dogs (perhaps 30%) may not respond to vaccination.

Borrelia burgdorferi: The cause of Lyme disease, the risk of which varies with the geographic area in which the pet lives and travels. Lyme disease is spread by deer ticks in the eastern US and western black-legged ticks in the western part of the country, and the risk of exposure is high in some regions. Lameness, fever and inappetence are most commonly seen in affected dogs. The extent of protection from the vaccine has not been conclusively demonstrated.

Coronavirus: This disease has a high risk of exposure, especially in areas where dogs congregate, but it typically causes only mild to moderate digestive upset (diarrhea, vomiting, etc.). Vaccines are available, but the duration of protection is believed to be relatively short and the effectiveness of the vaccine in preventing infection is considered low.

There are many other vaccinations available, including those for *Giardia* and canine adenovirus-1. While there may be some specific indications for their use, and local risk factors to be considered, they are not widely recommended for most dogs.

decision about the best way to protect pets through vaccination.

Years ago, it was just accepted that puppies got a starter series of vaccinations and then annual "boosters" throughout their lives to keep them protected. As more and more vaccines became available, consumers wanted the convenience of having all of that protection in a single injection. The result was "multivalent" vaccines that crammed a lot of protection into a single syringe. The manufacturers' recommendations were to give the vaccines annually, and this was a simple enough protocol to follow. However, as veterinary medicine has become more sophisticated and we have started looking more at healthcare quandaries rather than convenience, it became necessary to reevaluate the situation and deal with some tough questions. It is important to realize that whether or not to use a particular vaccine depends on the risk of contracting the disease against which it protects, the severity of the disease if it is contracted, the duration of immunity provided by the vaccine, the safety of the product and the needs of the individual animal. In a very general sense, rabies, distemper, hepatitis and parvovirus are considered core vaccine needs, while parainfluenza, *Bordctclla bronchiseptica*, leptospirosis, coronavirus and borreliosis (Lyme disease) are considered non-core

needs and best reserved for animals that demonstrate reasonable risk of contracting the diseases.

NEUTERING/SPAYING

Sterilization procedures (neutering for males/spaying for females) are meant to accomplish several purposes. While the underlying premise is to address the risk of pet overpopulation, there are also some medical and behavioral benefits to the surgeries as well. For females, spaying prior to the first estrus (heat cycle) leads to a marked reduction in the risk of mammary cancer. There also will be no manifestations of "heat" to attract male dogs and no bleeding in the house. For males, there is prevention of testicular cancer and a reduction in the risk of prostate problems. In both sexes, there may be some limited reduction in aggressive behaviors toward other dogs, and some diminishing of urine marking, roaming and mounting.

While neutering and spaying do indeed prevent animals from contributing to pet overpopulation, even no-cost and low-cost neutering options have not eliminated the problem. Perhaps one of the main reasons for this is that individuals that intentionally breed their dogs and those that allow their animals to run at large are the main causes of unwanted offspring. Also, animals in shelters are often there because they were abandoned or relinquished, not because they came from unplanned matings. Neutering/spaying is important, but it should be considered in the context of the real causes of animals' ending up in shelters and eventually being euthanized.

One of the important considerations regarding neutering is that it is a surgical procedure. This sometimes gets lost in discussions of low-cost procedures and commoditization of the process. In females, spaying is specifically referred to as an ovariohysterectomy. In this procedure, a midline incision is made in the abdomen and the entire uterus and both ovaries are surgically removed. While this is a major invasive surgical procedure, it usually has few complications, because it is typically performed on healthy young animals. However, it is major surgery, as any woman who has had a hysterectomy will attest.

In males, neutering has traditionally referred to castration, which involves the surgical removal of both testicles. While still a significant piece of surgery, there is not the abdominal exposure that is required in the female surgery. In addition, there is now a chemical sterilization option, in which a solution is injected into each testicle, leading to atrophy of the sperm-producing cells. This can typically be done under sedation rather than full anesthesia. This is a relatively new approach, and there are no long-term clinical studies yet available.

Neutering/spaying is typically done around six months of age at most veterinary hospitals, although techniques have been pioneered to perform the procedures in animals as young as eight weeks of age. In general, the surgeries on the very young animals are done for the specific reason of sterilizing them before they go to their new homes. This is done in some shelter hospitals for assurance that the animals will definitely not produce any pups. Otherwise, these organizations need to rely on owners to comply with their wishes to have the animals "altered" at a later date, something that does not always happen.

DOGGIE DENTAL DON'TS

A veterinary dental exam is necessary if you notice one or any combination of the following in your dog:

• Broken, loose or missing teeth
• Loss of appetite (which could be due to mouth pain or illness caused by infection)
• Gum abnormalities, including redness, swelling and bleeding
• Drooling, with or without blood
• Yellowing of the teeth or gumline, indicating tartar
• Bad breath

THE **ABC**s OF
Emergency Care

Abrasions
Clean wound with running water or 3% hydrogen peroxide. Pat dry with gauze and spray with antibiotic. Do not cover.

Animal Bites
Clean area with soap and saline solution or water. Apply pressure to any bleeding area. Apply antibiotic ointment.

Antifreeze Poisoning
Induce vomiting and take dog to the vet.

Bee Sting
Remove stinger and apply soothing lotion or cold compress; give antihistamine in proper dosage.

Bleeding
Apply pressure directly to wound with gauze or towel for five to ten minutes. If wound does not stop bleeding, wrap wound with gauze and adhesive tape.

Bloat/Gastric Torsion
Immediately take the dog to the vet or emergency clinic; phone from car. No time to waste.

Burns
Chemical: Bathe dog with water and pet shampoo. Rinse in saline solution. Apply antibiotic ointment.

Acid: Rinse with water. Apply one part baking soda, two parts water to affected area.

Alkali: Rinse with water. Apply one part vinegar, four parts water to affected area.

Electrical: Apply antibiotic ointment. Seek veterinary assistance immediately.

Choking
If the dog is on the verge of collapsing, wedge a solid object, such as the handle of screwdriver, between molars on one side of mouth to keep mouth open. Pull tongue out. Use long-nosed pliers or fingers to remove foreign object. Do not push the object down the dog's throat. For small or medium dogs, hold dog upside down by hind legs and shake firmly to dislodge foreign object.

Chlorine Ingestion
With clean water, rinse the mouth and eyes. Give dog water to drink; contact the vet.

Constipation
Feed dog 2 tablespoons bran flakes with each meal. Encourage drinking water. Mix 1/4 teaspoon mineral oil in dog's food.

Diarrhea
Withhold food for 12 to 24 hours. Feed dog anti-diarrheal with eyedropper. When feeding resumes, feed one part boiled hamburger, one part plain cooked rice, 1/4 to 3/4-cup four times daily.

Dog Bite
Snip away hair around puncture wound; clean with 3% hydrogen peroxide; apply tincture of iodine. If wound appears deep, take the dog to the vet.

Frostbite
Wrap the dog in a heavy blanket. Warm affected area with a warm bath for ten minutes. Red color to skin will return with circulation; if tissues are pale after 20 minutes, contact the vet.

Use a portable, durable container large enough to contain all items

Heat Stroke
Submerge the dog in cold water; if no response within ten minutes, contact the vet.

Hot Spots
Mix 2 packets Domeboro® with 2 cups water. Saturate cloth with mixture and apply to hot spots for 15–30 minutes. Apply antibiotic ointment. Repeat every six to eight hours.

Poisonous Plants
Wash affected area with soap and water. Cleanse with alcohol. For foxtail/grass, apply antibiotic ointment.

Rat Poison Ingestion
Induce vomiting. Keep dog calm, maintain dog's normal body temperature (use blanket or heating pad). Get to the vet for antidote.

Shock
Keep the dog calm and warm; call for veterinary assistance.

Snake Bite
If possible, bandage the area and apply pressure. If the area is not conducive to bandaging, use ice to control bleeding. Get immediate help from the vet.

Tick Removal
Apply flea and tick spray directly on tick. Wait one minute. Using tweezers or wearing plastic gloves, grasp the tick's body firmly. Apply antibiotic ointment.

Vomiting
Restrict dog's water intake; offer a few ice cubes. Withhold food for next meal. Contact vet if vomiting persists longer than 24 hours.

DOG OWNER'S FIRST-AID KIT
- ❏ **Gauze bandages/swabs**
- ❏ **Adhesive and non-adhesive bandages**
- ❏ **Antibiotic powder**
- ❏ **Antiseptic wash**
- ❏ **Hydrogen peroxide 3%**
- ❏ **Antibiotic ointment**
- ❏ **Lubricating jelly**
- ❏ **Rectal thermometer**
- ❏ **Nylon muzzle**
- ❏ **Scissors and forceps**
- ❏ **Eyedropper**
- ❏ **Syringe**
- ❏ **Anti-bacterial/fungal solution**
- ❏ **Saline solution**
- ❏ **Antihistamine**
- ❏ **Cotton balls**
- ❏ **Nail clippers**
- ❏ **Screwdriver/pen knife**
- ❏ **Flashlight**
- ❏ **Emergency phone numbers**

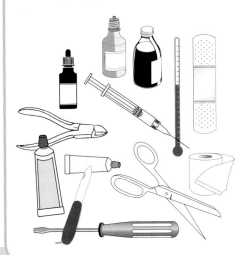

S. E. M. by Dr. Dennis Kunkel, University of Hawaii.

A scanning electron micrograph of a dog flea, Ctenocephalides canis, on dog hair.

EXTERNAL PARASITES

FLEAS

Fleas have been around for millions of years and, while we have better tools now for controlling them than at any time in the past, there still is little chance that they will end up on an endangered species list. Actually, they are very well adapted to living on our pets, and they continue to adapt as we make advances.

The female flea can consume 15 times her weight in blood during active reproduction and can lay as many as 40 eggs a day. These eggs are very resistant to the effects of insecticides. They hatch into larvae, which then mature and spin cocoons. The immature fleas reside in this pupal stage until the time is right for feeding. This pupal stage is also very resistant to the effects of insecticides, and pupae can last in the environment without feeding for many months. Newly emergent fleas are attracted to animals by the warmth of the animals' bodies, movement and exhaled carbon dioxide. However, when they first emerge from their cocoons, they orient towards light; thus when an animal passes between a flea and the light source, casting a shadow, the flea pounces and starts to feed. If the animal turns out to be a dog or cat, the reproductive cycle continues. If the flea lands on another type of animal, including a person, the flea will bite but will then look for a more appropriate host. An emerging adult flea can survive without feeding for up to 12 months but, once it tastes blood, it can survive off its host for only three to four days.

It was once thought that fleas spend most of their lives in the environment, but we now know that fleas won't willingly jump off a dog unless leaping to another dog or when physically removed by brushing, bathing or other manipulation. Flea eggs, on the other hand, are shiny and smooth, and they roll off the animal and into the environment. The eggs, larvae and pupae then exist in the environment, but once the adult finds a susceptible animal, it's home sweet home until the flea is forced to seek refuge elsewhere.

Since adult fleas live on the animal and immature forms survive in the environment, a successful treatment plan must address all stages of the flea life cycle. There are now several safe and effective flea-control products that can be applied on a monthly

FLEA PREVENTION FOR YOUR DOG

- Discuss with your veterinarian the safest product to protect your dog, likely in the form of a monthly tablet or a liquid preparation placed on the back of the dog's neck.
- For dogs suffering from flea-bite dermatitis, a shampoo or topical insecticide treatment is required.
- Your lawn and property should be sprayed with an insecticide designed to kill fleas and ticks that lurk outdoors.
- Using a flea comb, check the dog's coat regularly for any signs of parasites.
- Practice good housekeeping. Vacuum floors, carpets and furniture regularly, especially in the areas that the dog frequents, and wash the dog's bedding weekly.
- Follow up house-cleaning with carpet shampoos and sprays to rid the house of fleas at all stages of development. Insect growth regulators are the safest option.

basis. These include fipronil, imidacloprid, selamectin and permethrin (found in several formulations). Most of these products have significant flea-killing rates within 24 hours. However, none of them will control the immature forms in the environment. To accomplish this, there are a variety of insect growth regulators that can be sprayed into

THE FLEA'S LIFE CYCLE

What came first, the flea or the egg? This age-old mystery is more difficult to comprehend than the

actual cycle of the flea. Fleas usually live only about four months. A female can lay 2,000 eggs in her lifetime.

Egg

Photo by Carolina Biological Supply Co.

After ten days of rolling around your carpet or under your furniture, the eggs hatch into larvae,

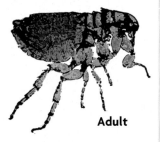

Larva

Photo by Carolina Biological Supply Co.

which feed on various and sundry debris. In days or

months, depending on the climate, the larvae spin cocoons and develop into the pupal or nymph stage, which quickly develop into fleas.

Pupa

These immature fleas must locate a host within 10 to 14 days or they will die. Only about 1% of the flea population exist as adult fleas, while the other 99% exist as eggs, larvae or pupae.

Adult

KILL FLEAS THE NATURAL WAY

If you choose not to go the route of conventional medication, there are some natural ways to ward off fleas:

- Dust your dog with a natural flea powder, composed of such herbal goodies as rosemary, wormwood, pennyroyal, citronella, rue, tobacco powder and eucalyptus.
- Apply diatomaceous earth, the fossilized remains of single-cell algae, to your carpets, furniture and pet's bedding. Even though it's not good for dogs, it's even worse for fleas, which will dry up swiftly and die.
- Brush your dog frequently, give him adequate exercise and let him fast occasionally. All of these activities strengthen the dog's system and make him more resistant to disease and parasites.
- Bathe your dog with a capful of pennyroyal or eucalyptus oil.
- Feed a natural diet, free of additives and preservatives. Add some fresh garlic and brewer's yeast to the dog's morning portion, as these items have flea-repelling properties.

the environment (e.g., pyriprox-yfen, methoprene, fenoxycarb) as well as insect development inhibitors such as lufenuron that can be administered. These compounds have no effect on adult fleas, but they stop imma-ture forms from developing into

adults. In years gone by, we relied heavily on toxic insecticides (such as organophosphates, organochlo-rines and carbamates) to manage the flea problem, but today's options are not only much safer to use on our pets but also safer for the environment.

TICKS

Ticks are members of the spider class (arachnids) and are blood-sucking parasites capable of transmitting a variety of diseases, including Lyme disease, ehrlichiosis, babesiosis and Rocky Mountain spotted fever. It's easy to see ticks on your own skin, but it is more of a challenge when your furry companion is affected. Whenever you happen to be planning a stroll in a tick-infested area (especially forests, grassy or wooded areas or parks) be prepared to do a thorough inspection of your dog afterward to search for ticks. Ticks can be tricky, so make sure you spend time looking in the ears, between the toes and everywhere else where a tick might hide. Ticks need to be attached for 24–72 hours before they transmit most of the diseases that they carry, so you do have a window of opportunity for some preventive intervention.

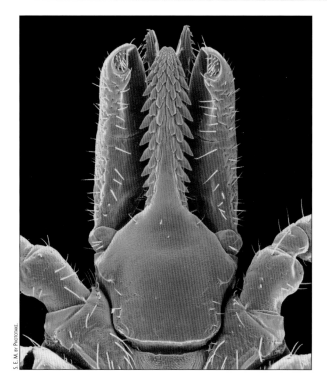

S. E. M. BY PHOTOTAKE.

A scanning electron micrograph of the head of a female deer tick, *Ixodes dammini*, a parasitic tick that carries Lyme disease.

A TICKING BOMB

There is nothing good about a tick's harpooning his nose into your dog's skin. Among the diseases caused by ticks are Rocky Mountain spotted fever, canine ehrlichiosis, canine babesiosis, canine hepatozoonosis and Lyme disease. If a dog is allergic to the saliva of a female wood tick, he can develop tick paralysis.

Female ticks live to eat and breed. They can lay between 4,000 and 5,000 eggs and they die soon after. Males, on the other hand, live only to mate with the females and continue the process as long as they are able. Most ticks live on multiple hosts before parasitizing dogs. The immature forms typically reside on grass and shrubs, waiting for susceptible animals to walk by. The larvae and nymph stages typically feed on wildlife.

If only a few ticks are present on a dog, they can be plucked out, but it is important to remove the entire head and mouthparts,

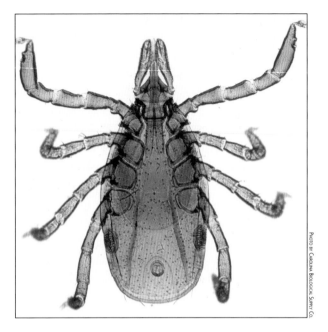

PHOTO BY CAROLINA BIOLOGICAL SUPPLY CO.

Deer tick,
Ixodes dammini.

of in a container of alcohol or household bleach.

Some of the newer flea products, specifically those with fipronil, selamectin and permethrin, have effect against some, but not all, species of tick. Flea collars containing appropriate pesticides (e.g., propoxur, chlorfenvinphos) can aid in tick control. In most areas, such collars should be placed on animals in March, at the beginning of the tick season, and changed regularly. Leaving the collar on when the pesticide level is waning invites the development of resistance. Amitraz collars are also good for tick control, and the active ingredient does not interfere with other flea-control products. The ingredient helps prevent the attachment of ticks to the skin and will cause those ticks already on the skin to detach themselves.

which may be deeply embedded in the skin. This is best accomplished with forceps designed especially for this purpose; fingers can be used but should be protected with rubber gloves, plastic wrap or at least a paper towel. The tick should be grasped as closely as possible to the animal's skin and should be pulled upward with steady, even pressure. Do not squeeze, crush or puncture the body of the tick or you risk exposure to any disease carried by that tick. Once the ticks have been removed, the sites of attachment should be disinfected. Your hands should then be washed with soap and water to further minimize risk of contagion. The tick should be disposed

TICK CONTROL

Removal of underbrush and leaf litter and the thinning of trees in areas where tick control is desired are recommended. These actions remove the cover and food sources for small animals that serve as hosts for ticks. With continued mowing of grasses in these areas, the probability of ticks' surviving is further reduced. A variety of insecticide ingredients (e.g., resmethrin, carbaryl, permethrin, chlorpyrifos, dioxathion and allethrin) are registered for tick control around the home.

MITES

Mites are tiny arachnid parasites that parasitize the skin of dogs. Skin diseases caused by mites are referred to as "mange," and there are many different forms seen in dogs. These forms are very different from one another, each one warranting an individual description.

Sarcoptic mange, or scabies, is one of the itchiest conditions that affects dogs. The microscopic *Sarcoptes* mites burrow into the superficial layers of the skin and can drive dogs crazy with itchiness. They are also communicable to people, although they can't complete their reproductive cycle on people. In addition to being tiny, the mites also are often difficult to find when trying to make a diagnosis. Skin scrapings from multiple areas are examined microscopically but, even then, sometimes the mites cannot be found.

Fortunately, scabies is relatively easy to treat, and there are a variety of products that will successfully kill the mites. Since the mites can't live in the environment for very long without feeding, a complete cure is usually possible within four to eight weeks.

Cheyletiellosis is caused by a relatively large mite, which sometimes can be seen even without a microscope. Often referred to as "walking dandruff," this also causes itching, but not usually as profound as with scabies. While *Cheyletiella*

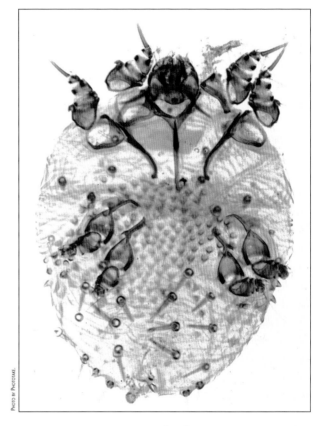

PHOTO BY PHOTOTAKE.

mites can survive somewhat longer in the environment than scabies mites, they too are relatively easy to treat, being responsive to not only the medications used to treat scabies but also often to flea-control products.

Otodectes cynotis is the canine ear mite and is one of the more common causes of mange, especially in young dogs in shelters or pet stores. That's because the mites are typically present in large numbers and are quickly spread to nearby animals. The mites rarely do

Sarcoptes scabiei, commonly known as the "itch mite."

Micrograph of a dog louse, *Heterodoxus spiniger*. Female lice attach their eggs to the hairs of the dog. As the eggs hatch, the larval lice bite and feed on the blood. Lice can also feed on dead skin and hair. This feeding activity can cause hair loss and skin problems.

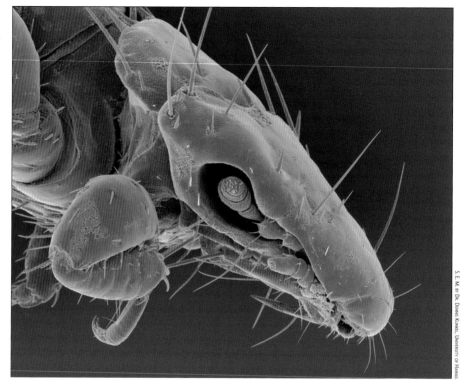

S. E. M. BY DR. DENNIS KUNKEL, UNIVERSITY OF HAWAII

much harm but can be difficult to eradicate if the treatment regimen is not comprehensive. While many try to treat the condition with ear drops only, this is the most common cause of treatment failure. Ear drops cause the mites to simply move out of the ears and as far away as possible (usually to the base of the tail) until the insecticide levels in the ears drop to an acceptable level—then it's back to business as usual! The successful treatment of ear mites requires treating all animals in the household with a systemic insecticide, such as selamectin, or a combination of miticidal ear drops combined with whole-body flea-control preparations.

Demodicosis, sometimes referred to as red mange, can be one of the most difficult forms of mange to treat. Part of the problem has to do with the fact that the mites live in the hair follicles and they are relatively well shielded from topical and systemic products. The main issue, however, is that demodectic mange typically results only when there is some underlying process interfering with the dog's immune system.

Since *Demodex* mites are normal residents of the skin of

mammals, including humans, there is usually a mite population explosion only when the immune system fails to keep the number of mites in check. In young animals, the immune deficit may be transient or may reflect an actual inherited immune problem. In older animals, demodicosis is usually seen only when there is another disease hampering the immune system, such as diabetes, cancer, thyroid problems or the use of immune-suppressing drugs. Accordingly, treatment involves not only trying to kill the mange mites but also discerning what is interfering with immune function and correcting it if possible.

Chiggers represent several different species of mite that don't parasitize dogs specifically, but do latch on to passersby and can cause irritation. The problem is most prevalent in wooded areas in the late summer and fall. Treatment is not difficult, as the mites do not complete their life cycle on dogs and are susceptible to a variety of miticidal products.

MOSQUITOES

Mosquitoes have long been known to transmit a variety of diseases to people, as well as just being biting pests during warm weather. They also pose a real risk to pets. Not only do they carry deadly heartworms but

ILLUSTRATION BY PHOTOTAKE.

Illustration of Demodex folliculoram.

recently there also has been much concern over their involvement with West Nile virus. While we can avoid heartworm with the use of preventive medications, there are no such preventives for West Nile virus. The only method of prevention in endemic areas is active mosquito control. Fortunately, most dogs that have been exposed to the virus only developed flu-like symptoms and, to date, there have not been the large number of reported deaths in canines as seen in some other species.

MOSQUITO REPELLENT

Low concentrations of DEET (less than 10%), found in many human mosquito repellents, have been safely used in dogs but, in these concentrations, probably give only about two hours of protection. DEET may be safe in these small concentrations, but since it is not licensed for use on dogs, there is no research proving its safety for dogs. Products containing permethrin give the longest-lasting protection, perhaps two to four weeks. As DEET is not licensed for use on dogs, and both DEET and permethrin can be quite toxic to cats, appropriate care should be exercised. Other products, such as those containing oil of citronella, also have some mosquito-repellent activity, but typically have a relatively short duration of action.

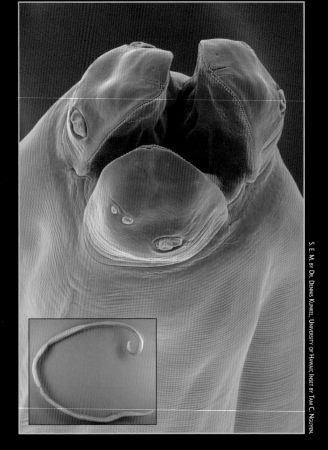

S. E. M. BY DR. DENNIS KUNKEL, UNIVERSITY OF HAWAII. INSET BY TAM C. NGUYEN.

The ascarid roundworm *Toxocara canis*, showing the mouth with three lips. INSET: Photomicrograph of the roundworm *Ascaris lumbricoides.*

INTERNAL PARASITES: WORMS

ASCARIDS

Ascarids are intestinal roundworms that rarely cause severe disease in dogs. Nonetheless, they are of major public health significance because they can be transferred to people. Sadly, it is children who are most commonly affected by the parasite, probably from inadvertently ingesting ascarid-contaminated soil. In fact, many yards and children's sandboxes contain appreciable numbers of ascarid eggs. So, while ascarids don't bite dogs or latch onto their intestines to suck blood, they do cause some nasty medical conditions in children and are best eradicated from our furry friends. Because pups can start passing ascarid eggs by three weeks of age, most parasite-control programs begin at two weeks of age and are repeated every two weeks until pups are eight weeks old. It is important to

HOOKED ON ANCYLOSTOMA

Adult dogs can become infected by the bloodsucking nematodes we commonly call hookworms via ingesting larvae from the ground or via the larvae penetrating the dog's skin. It is not uncommon for infected dogs to show no symptoms of hookworm infestation. Sometimes symptoms occur within ten days of exposure. These symptoms can include bloody diarrhea, anemia, loss of weight and general weakness. Dogs pass the hookworm eggs in their stools, which serves as the vet's method of identifying the infestation. The hookworm larvae can encyst themselves in the dog's tissues and be released when the dog is experiencing stress.

Caused by an *Ancylostoma* species whose common host is the dog, cutaneous larval migrans affects humans, causing itching and lumps and streaks beneath the surface of the skin.

S. E. M. BY DR. DENNIS KUNKEL, UNIVERSITY OF HAWAII.

realize that bitches can pass ascarids to their pups even if they test negative prior to whelping. Accordingly, bitches are best treated at the same time as the pups.

HOOKWORMS

Unlike ascarids, hookworms do latch onto a dog's intestinal tract and can cause significant loss of blood and protein. Similar to ascarids, hookworms can be transmitted to humans, where they cause a condition known as cutaneous larval migrans. Dogs can become infected either by consuming the infective larvae or by the larvae's penetrating the skin directly. People most often get infected when they are lying on the ground (such as on a beach) and the larvae penetrate the skin. Yes, the larvae can penetrate through a beach blanket. Hookworms are typically susceptible to the same medications used to treat ascarids.

The hookworm *Ancylostoma caninum* infests the intestines of dogs. INSET: Note the row of hooks at the posterior end, used to anchor the worm to the intestinal wall.

WHIPWORMS

Whipworms latch onto the lower aspects of the dog's colon and can cause cramping and diarrhea. Eggs do not start to appear in the dog's feces until about three months after the dog was infected. This worm has a peculiar life cycle, which makes it more difficult to control than ascarids or hookworms. The good thing is that whipworms rarely are transferred to people.

Some of the medications used to treat ascarids and hookworms are also effective against whipworms, but, in general, a separate treatment protocol is needed. Since most of the medications are effective against the adults but not the eggs or larvae, treatment is typically repeated in three weeks, and then often in three

months as well. Unfortunately, since dogs don't develop resistance to whipworms, it is difficult to prevent them from getting reinfected if they visit soil contaminated with whipworm eggs.

WORM-CONTROL GUIDELINES

- Practice sanitary habits with your dog and home.
- Clean up after your dog and don't let him sniff or eat other dogs' droppings.
- Control insects and fleas in the dog's environment. Fleas, lice, cockroaches, beetles, mice and rats can act as hosts for various worms.
- Prevent dogs from eating uncooked meat, raw poultry and dead animals.
- Keep dogs and children from playing in sand and soil.
- Kennel dogs on cement or gravel; avoid dirt runs.
- Administer heartworm preventives regularly.
- Have your vet examine your dog's stools at your annual visits.
- Select a boarding kennel carefully so as to avoid contamination from other dogs or an unsanitary environment.
- Prevent dogs from roaming. Obey local leash laws.

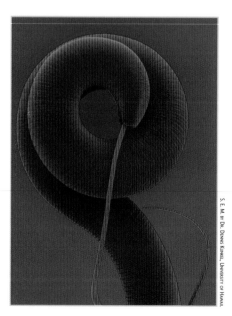

Adult whipworm, *Trichuris* sp., an intestinal parasite.

S. E. M. BY DR. DENNIS KUNKEL, UNIVERSITY OF HAWAII

TAPEWORMS

There are many different species of tapeworm that affect dogs, but *Dipylidium caninum* is probably the most common and is spread by fleas. Flea larvae feed on organic debris and tapeworm eggs in the environment and, when a dog chews at himself and manages to ingest fleas, he might get a dose of tapeworm at the same time. The tapeworm then develops further in the intestine of the dog.

The tapeworm itself, which is a parasitic flatworm that latches onto the intestinal wall, is composed of numerous segments. When the segments break off into the intestine (as proglottids), they may accumulate around the rectum, like grains of rice. While this tapeworm is disgusting in its behavior, it is not directly communicable to humans (although humans can also get infected by swallowing fleas).

A much more dangerous flatworm is *Echinococcus multilocularis*, which is typically found in foxes, coyotes and wolves. The eggs are passed in the feces and infect rodents, and, when dogs eat the rodents, the dogs can be infected by thousands of adult tapeworms. While the parasites don't cause many problems in dogs, this is considered the most lethal worm infection that people can get. Take appropriate precautions if you live in an area in which these tapeworms are found. Do not use mulch that may contain feces of dogs, cats or wildlife, and discourage your pets from hunting wildlife. Treat these tapeworm infections aggressively in pets, because if humans get infected, approximately half die.

HEARTWORMS

Heartworm disease is caused by the parasite *Dirofilaria immitis* and is seen in dogs around the world. A member of the roundworm group, it is spread between dogs by the bite of an infected mosquito. The mosquito injects infective larvae into the dog's skin with its bite, and these larvae develop under the skin for a period of time before making their way to the heart. There they develop into adults, which grow and create blockages of the heart, lungs and major blood vessels there. They also start producing offspring (microfilariae)

A dog tapeworm proglottid (body segment).

The dog tapeworm *Taenia pisiformis.*

A Look at Internal Parasites

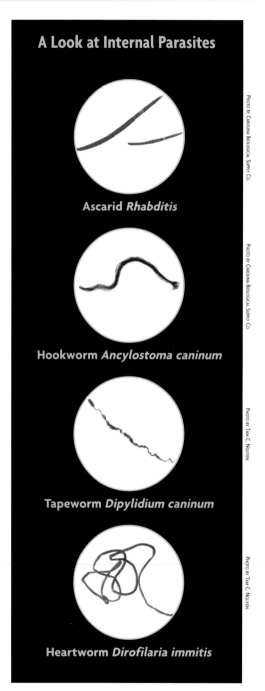

Ascarid *Rhabditis*

PHOTO BY CAROLINA BIOLOGICAL SUPPLY CO.

Hookworm *Ancylostoma caninum*

PHOTO BY CAROLINA BIOLOGICAL SUPPLY CO.

Tapeworm *Dipylidium caninum*

PHOTO BY TAM C. NGUYEN

Heartworm *Dirofilaria immitis*

PHOTO BY TAM C. NGUYEN

and these microfilariae circulate in the bloodstream, waiting to hitch a ride when the next mosquito bites. Once in the mosquito, the microfilariae develop into infective larvae and the entire process is repeated.

When dogs get infected with heartworm, over time they tend to develop symptoms associated with heart disease, such as coughing, exercise intolerance and potentially many other manifestations. Diagnosis is confirmed by either seeing the microfilariae themselves in blood samples or using immunologic tests (antigen testing) to identify the presence of adult heartworms. Since antigen tests measure the presence of adult heartworms and microfilarial tests measure offspring produced by adults, neither are positive until six to seven months after the initial infection. However, the beginning of damage can occur by fifth-stage larvae as early as three months after infection. Thus it is possible for dogs to be harboring problem-causing larvae for up to three months before either type of test would identify an infection.

The good news is that there are great protocols available for preventing heartworm in dogs. Testing is critical in the process, and it is important to understand the benefits as well as the limitations of such testing. All dogs six months of age or older that have not been on continuous heartworm-preventive medication should be

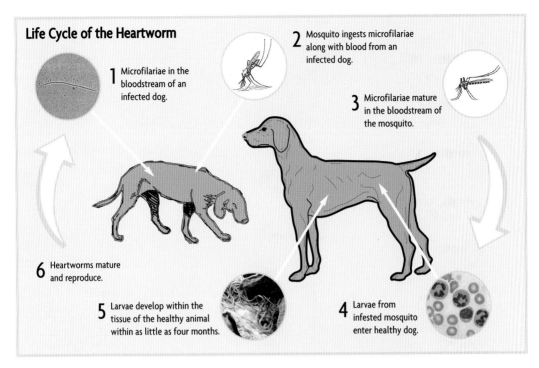

Life Cycle of the Heartworm

1 Microfilariae in the bloodstream of an infected dog.

2 Mosquito ingests microfilariae along with blood from an infected dog.

3 Microfilariae mature in the bloodstream of the mosquito.

6 Heartworms mature and reproduce.

5 Larvae develop within the tissue of the healthy animal within as little as four months.

4 Larvae from infested mosquito enter healthy dog.

screened with microfilarial or antigen tests. For dogs receiving preventive medication, periodic antigen testing helps assess the effectiveness of the preventives. The American Heartworm Society guidelines suggest that annual retesting may not be necessary when owners have absolutely provided continuous heartworm prevention. Retesting on a two- to three-year interval may be sufficient in these cases. However, your veterinarian will likely have specific guidelines under which heartworm preventives will be prescribed, and many prefer to err on the side of safety and retest annually.

It is indeed fortunate that heartworm is relatively easy to prevent, because treatments can be as life-threatening as the disease itself. Treatment requires a two-step process that kills the adult heartworms first and then the microfilariae. Prevention is obviously preferable; this involves a once-monthly oral or topical treatment. The most common oral preventives include ivermectin (not suitable for some breeds), moxidectin and milbemycin oxime; the once-a-month topical drug selamectin provides heartworm protection in addition to flea, tick and other parasite controls.

BOUVIER DES FLANDRES

If you are considering entering your Bouvier des Flandres in a dog show, here are some basic questions to ask yourself:

- Did you purchase a "show-quality" puppy from the breeder?
- Is your puppy at least six months of age?
- Does the puppy exhibit correct show type for his breed?
- Does your puppy have any disqualifying faults?
- Is your Bouvier des Flandres registered with the American Kennel Club?
- How much time do you have to devote to training, grooming, conditioning and exhibiting your dog?
- Do you understand the rules and regulations of a dog show?
- Do you have time to learn how to show your dog properly?

- Do you have the financial resources to invest in showing your dog?
- Will you show the dog yourself or hire a professional handler?
- Do you have a vehicle that can accommodate your weekend trips to the dog shows?

Success in the show ring requires more than a pretty face, a waggy tail and a pocketful of liver. Even though dog shows can be exciting and enjoyable, the sport of conformation makes great demands on the exhibitors and the dogs. Winning exhibitors live for their dogs, devoting time and money to their dogs' presentation, conditioning and training. Very few novices, even those with good dogs, will find themselves in the winners' circle, though it does happen. Don't be disheartened, though. Every exhibitor began as a novice and worked his way up to the Group ring. It's the "working your way up" part that you must keep in mind.

AKC CONFORMATION

How do you acquaint yourself with conformation showing?

AKC GROUPS

For showing purposes, the AKC divides its recognized breeds into seven groups: Sporting Dogs, Hounds, Working Dogs, Terriers, Toys, Non-Sporting Dogs and Herding Dogs. The Bouvier is in the Herding Group.

Visiting a dog show as a spectator is a great place to start. Pick up the show catalog to find out what time your breed is being shown, who is judging the breed and in which ring the classes will be held. To start, Bouviers des Flandres compete against other Bouviers des Flandres, and the winner is selected as Best of Breed by the judge. This is the procedure for each breed. At a group show, all of the Best of Breed winners go on to compete for Group One in their respective groups. For example, all Best of Breed winners in a given group compete against each other; this is done for all seven groups. Finally, all seven group winners go head to head in the ring for the Best in Show award.

What most spectators don't understand is the basic idea of conformation. A dog show is often referred to as a "conformation" show. This means that the judge should decide how each dog stacks up (conforms) to the breed standard for his given breed: how well does this Bouvier des Flandres conform to the ideal representative detailed in the standard? Ideally, this is what happens. In reality, however, this ideal often gets slighted as the judge compares Bouvier des Flandres #1 to Bouvier des Flandres #2. Again, the ideal is that each dog is judged based on his merits in comparison to his breed standard, not in comparison

to the other dogs in the ring. It is easier for judges to compare dogs of the same breed to decide which they think is the better specimen; in the Group and Best in Show ring, however, it is very difficult to compare one breed to another, like apples to oranges. Thus the dog's conformation to the breed standard—not to mention advertising dollars and good handling—is essential to success in conformation shows. The dog described in the standard (the standard for each AKC breed is written and approved by the breed's national parent club and then submitted to the AKC for approval) is the perfect dog of that breed, and breeders keep their eye on the standard when they choose which dogs to breed, hoping to get closer and closer to the ideal with each litter.

Another good first step for the novice is to join a dog club.

Before entering the ring, you and your dog should have a basic idea of what you're doing. This youngster practices his show pose at home with his owner.

Dog clubs may specialize in a single breed, like a local or regional Bouvier des Flandres club, or in a specific pursuit, such as obedience, tracking or herding tests. There are all-breed clubs and also clubs that specialize in certain types of dogs, like herding dogs, hunting dogs, companion dogs, etc.

A parent club is the national organization, sanctioned by the AKC, which promotes and safeguards its breed in the country. The American Bouvier des Flandres Club of America was formed in 1963 and can be contacted on the Internet at www.bouvier.org. The parent club holds annual national specialty shows, for the Bouvier only, usually in different regions of the country in which many of the top dogs, handlers and breeders

Dutch and American Champion Tino Faisca v.d. Vanenblikhoeve has had some impressive wins, including the top prize at the Dutch national specialty.

> **BECOMING A CHAMPION**
> An official AKC championship of record requires that a dog accumulate 15 points under three different judges, including two "majors" under different judges. Points are awarded based on the number of dogs entered into competition, varying from breed to breed and place to place. A win of three, four or five points is considered a "major." The AKC annually assigns a schedule of points to adjust for variations that accompany a breed's popularity and the population of a given area.

gather to compete. For more information about dog clubs in your area, contact the AKC at www.akc.org on the Internet or write them at 5580 Centerview Drive, Raleigh, NC 27606.

OBEDIENCE TRIALS
Obedience exercises were originally intended to evaluate the working relationship between dog and owner. Since those early days of the sport in the US, obedience trials have grown more and more popular, and now more than 2,000 trials each year attract over 100,000 dogs and their owners. Any dog registered with the AKC, regardless of neutering or other disqualifications that would preclude entry in conformation competition, can participate in obedience trials.

There are three levels of difficulty in obedience competition. The first (and easiest) level is the Novice, in which dogs can earn the Companion Dog (CD) title. The intermediate level is the Open level, in which the Companion Dog Excellent (CDX) title is awarded. The advanced level is the Utility level, in which dogs compete for the Utility Dog (UD) title. Classes at each level are further divided into "A" and "B," with "A" for beginners and "B" for those with more experience. In order to win a title at a given level, a dog must earn three "legs." A "leg" is accomplished when a dog scores 170 or higher (200 is a perfect score). The scoring system gets a little trickier when you understand that a dog must score more than 50% of the points available for each exercise in order to actually earn the points. Available points for each exercise range between 20 and 40.

Once he's earned the UD title, a dog can go on to win the prestigious title of Utility Dog Excellent (UDX) by winning "legs" in ten shows. Additionally, Utility Dogs who win "legs" in Open B and Utility B earn points toward the lofty title of Obedience Trial Champion (OTCh.). Established in 1977 by the AKC, this title requires a dog to earn 100 points as well as three first places in a combination of Open B and Utility B classes under three different judges. The "brass ring" of obedience competition is the AKC's National Obedience Invitational. This is an exclusive competition for only the cream of the obedience crop. In order to qualify for the invitational, a dog must be ranked in either the top 25 all-breeds in obedience or in the top three for his breed in obedience. The title at stake here is that of National Obedience Champion (NOC).

AGILITY TRIALS

Agility trials became sanctioned by the AKC in August 1994, when the first licensed agility trials were held. Since that time, agility certainly has grown in popularity by leaps and bounds, literally! The AKC allows all registered

GETTING INTO AGILITY

Agility trials are a great way to keep your dog active, and they will keep you running too! You should join a local agility club to learn more about the sport. These clubs offer sessions in which you can introduce your dog to the various obstacles as well as training classes to prepare him for competition. In no time, your dog will be climbing A-frames, crossing the dog walk and flying over hurdles, all with you right beside him. Your heart will leap every time your dog jumps through the hoop—and you'll be having just as much (if not more) fun!

Proper movement means proper structure. Artful grooming won't be able to disguise conformational flaws, as a dog's gait reveals what's underneath.

breeds (including Miscellaneous Class breeds) to participate, providing the dog is 12 months of age or older. Agility is designed so that the handler demonstrates how well the dog can work at his side. The handler directs his dog through, over, under and around an obstacle course that includes jumps, tires, the dog walk, weave poles, pipe tunnels, collapsed tunnels and more. While working his way through the course, the dog must keep one eye and ear on the handler and the rest of his body on the course. The handler runs along with the dog, giving verbal and hand signals to guide the dog through the course.

The first organization to promote agility trials in the US was the United States Dog Agility Association, Inc. (USDAA). Established in 1986, the USDAA sparked the formation of many member clubs around the country. To participate in USDAA trials, dogs must be at least 18 months of age.

HERDING EVENTS
The first recorded sheepdog trial was held in Wales in the late 19th

TRACKING TESTS
Tracking tests are exciting ways to test your Bouvier des Flandres's instinctive scenting ability on a competitive level. All dogs have a nose, and all breeds are welcome in tracking tests. The first AKC-licensed tracking test took place in 1937 as part of the Utility level at an obedience trial, and thus competitive tracking was officially begun. The first title, Tracking Dog (TD), was offered in 1947, ten years after the first official tracking test. It was not until 1980 that the AKC added the title Tracking Dog Excellent (TDX), which was followed by the title Versatile Surface Tracking (VST) in 1995. Champion Tracker (CT) is awarded to a dog who has earned all three of those titles.

century; since then, the popularity of herding events has grown around the world. The AKC began offering herding events in 1989, and participation is open to all breeds in the Herding Group as well as Rottweilers and Samoyeds. These events are designed to evaluate the dogs' herding instincts, and the aim is to develop those innate skills and show that herding dogs today can still perform the functions for which they were originally intended, whether or not they are actually used in working capacities. Herding events are designed to simulate farm situations and are held on two levels: tests and trials.

AKC herding tests are more basic and are scored on a pass/fail system, meaning that dogs do not compete against each other to earn titles. Titles at this level are Herding Tested (HT) and the more difficult Pre-Trial Tested (PT). In addition, there is a non-competitive certification program, Herding Instinct Tested, which gives you a chance to evaluate the potential that your dog may have for herding. If your dog successfully passes this test, he receives a Herding Instinct Certificate, which makes him eligible to enter herding trials.

The more challenging herding trial level is competitive and requires more training and experience. There are three different courses (A, B and C, each with a different type of farm situation) with different types of livestock (cattle, sheep or ducks). There are three titles available on each course, Herding Started, Herding Intermediate and Herding Advanced, with each level being progressively more difficult. Handlers can choose the type of course and type of livestock for their dogs based on the breed's typical use. Once a Herding Advanced title has been earned on a course, the dog can then begin to strive for the Herding Champion title.

OTHER HERDING EVENTS

In addition to events held by the AKC, breed clubs often hold herding events for herding breeds. Other specialty organizations hold trials that are open to all herding breeds; the way these events are structured and the titles that are awarded differ from those of the AKC. For example, the American Herding Breed Association (AHBA) allows any breed with herding in its ancestry to participate, as well as allowing mixed-breed herding dogs. To pass the Herding Instinct Test, the handler works with the dog at the shepherd's direction while the shepherd evaluates the dog's willingness to approach, move and round up the sheep while at the same time following the instructions of his handler.

INDEX

My Bouvier des Flandres

PUT YOUR PUPPY'S FIRST PICTURE HERE

Dog's Name _____

Date _____ Photographer _____